THE
HOUSE OF COMMONS
AT WORK

*

Eric Taylor

PENGUIN BOOKS

HARMONDSWORTH · MIDDLESEX

Penguin Books Ltd, Harmondsworth, Middlesex

U.S.A.: Penguin Books Inc., 3300 Clipper Mill Road, Baltimore 11, Md
[*Educational Representative:*
D. C. Heath & Co, 285 Columbus Avenue, Boston 16, Mass]

AUSTRALIA: Penguin Books Pty Ltd, 200 Normanby Road,
Melbourne, S.C.5, Victoria

AGENT IN CANADA: Riverside Books Ltd, 47 Green Street,
Saint Lambert, Montreal, P.Q.

—

Collagravure plates printed by
Harrison and Sons Ltd, London

—

Made and printed in Great Britain by
Hunt, Barnard and Company Ltd, London and Aylesbury

—

F rst published 1951

CONTENTS

INTRODUCTION

PARLIAMENT, like the great Duke, might reasonably complain that it has of late been 'much exposed to authors'. Varying in scope and excellence from the fifteenth edition of Erskine May's *Parliamentary Practice* to the most trifling reminiscences, more books on this great institution have appeared in the last five years than probably the previous twenty years. It may safely be assumed that in these days of scarcity of men and materials so copious a supply must accurately reflect the urgency of the demand. Even without the appearance of these new books on Parliament, the vast increase in the sales of *Hansard*[1] and the long queues which every day wait patiently in rain and sun outside St Stephen's porch in the hope of admission to the Chamber are evidence enough of the new and intense interest in Parliament and matters parliamentary. It is undoubtedly a healthy interest. No one can deny that it is to the advantage of a democratic state that its members should be anxious to know as much as possible about the workings of their state and its Government. No one can deny that the desire for such knowledge should be as fully satisfied as possible. There is every possible justification for as great an abundance of books on this and related subjects as possible.

I do not, however, offer this work merely as a contribution to this desirable abundance. At the time when it was first projected (1943) there were hardly any books on the

1. The total daily issue of *Hansard* reached 12,100 copies in May 1946. The total issue of the '*Weekly Hansard*' reached a peak of 16,500 at that period, and although the figures have since declined, they are still very high. Up to 1944, the average sales of *Hansard* were less than 3,000.

7

procedure of Parliament which were not either out of date or unprocurable or both. The standard works on the subject, such as the great *Parliamentary Practice* of Erskine May, were frankly not designed for the general reader, even if they had been in print. I wished to provide an account of the procedure of the House of Commons – nothing more – which should be of a reasonable size, intelligible to the educated reader, and readable. I also wished it to be completely accurate in all its details, holding as I did that in a work which is a description of fact, accuracy was essential. It was not my desire to provide a 'child's guide to Parliament'. I considered it justifiable to assume a certain knowledge of fundamentals in my readers: for instance, that there are two Houses of Parliament, the one elected, and the other hereditary, and that the Government was selected by the Prime Minister from both Houses. On the other hand, I did not consider myself justified in assuming that the unprofessional reader was equipped with a much closer acquaintance with the facts than this. I wished to take him by the hand and guide rather than lead him through the intricacies – for they are intricacies – of parliamentary procedure.

A large section of the British public is probably unaware even of the existence of the procedure of the House of Commons. But an increasingly large number of people have become very much aware of it, through the reports of Parliament in the press and radio programmes. 'Who decides the programme of Parliament?' they ask, 'How long does Parliament sit? How many questions can an M.P. ask every day? How is the Speaker appointed? What is the Adjournment?' These and similar natural questions I felt needed an answer; and I attempted to answer them in this book. There was another kind of question which I also felt needed an answer – the question asked by the new Member of Parliament. 'How can I put down an amendment to a Bill? What opportunities will I have of speaking on this subject? How can I oppose this measure?' These questions also I set out to answer in this book.

Obviously, the position with regard to books on Parliament has greatly improved since this book was first projected. But I still feel that there is too great a gap between the sublime, formidable, almost unreadable excellence of books like Erskine May, and the jejune ebullience of the ordinary handbook on Parliament, so often grossly inaccurate, scandalously partisan, and, through its defect of dignity, almost as unreadable as May. At the same time, I felt it was necessary to write a readable book, not a book of reference. At all costs, I wished to avoid the long passive sentences and latinities which have become characteristic of procedural literature. I wished to avoid the use of words like 'mode' and 'deemed' which convey no meaning at all to the ordinary reader.

The method of approach which I have employed is perhaps unusual. The effect of the physical accidents of the chamber in which the House of Commons meets are undeniably great. I have, therefore, devoted a first chapter to describing it. But thereafter I have attempted to follow the ramification of the various parts of procedure from the firm basis of the formal motion. Though the procedure of the House of Commons is, like so many things English, to a great extent empirical, it is also ultimately based upon firmly held theoretical postulates: upon legal fictions which are almost as old as English history. It has seemed to me that it was in this way possible to bring to the study of procedure a greater unity of view than has usually been achieved in such works. Thus, though the material does not yield itself easily to literary graces, I hoped to produce a book which would combine pleasure with profit; and I hope that I have not been entirely unsuccessful.

It remains for me to express my deep sense of gratitude to the great writers upon procedure of the past, whose works I have pilfered, to Lord Campion, late Clerk of the House, to Commander Stephen King-Hall whose generous encouragement was primarily responsible for my attempting the book, as well as to those of my colleagues, especially Mr L. A. Abraham, C.B.E., and the late Mr St Clair Kingdom, who have so kindly revised the work and assisted me in various ways.

Chapter II was first published as an article in the *Quarterly Parliamentary Affairs*, four years ago.

CHAPTER I

THE CHAMBER AS IT WAS AND IS

The English Legislature, like the English people, is of slow temper, essentially conservative. In our wildest periods of reform, in the Long Parliament itself, you notice always the invincible instinct to hold fast by the Old; to admit the minimum of the New; to expand, if it be possible, some old habit or method, already found fruitful, into new growth for the new need. It is an instinct worthy of all honour; akin to all strength and all wisdom. The Future hereby is not dissevered from the Past, but based continuously on it; grows with all the vitalities of the Past, and is rooted down deep into the beginnings of us.

CARLYLE, Past and Present

In December 1943 a Select Committee was appointed to consider and report upon plans for the rebuilding of the House of Commons, and upon 'such alterations as may be considered desirable *while preserving all its essential features.*' For three years Members had endured the discomfort of various temporary chambers, since the terrible night of 10 May 1941, when German aircraft, dropping showers of incendiary bombs, attempted to destroy the entire Houses of Parliament. The bombers were unsuccessful in their attempt, but the actual chamber of the House of Commons, the scene of a century's political history, was destroyed. Nothing remained of it but the four walls, and heaps of twisted girders and charred timbers. Even in 1943 there were many who thought it was premature to begin the reconstruction. The position of Britain in the world conflict was by no means easy. Later on the rain of flying bombs was to force the Legislature to move again to a place of greater safety. But it was felt that the rebuilding would be a gesture of confidence in democracy: at any rate the Prime Minister thought so, and there were few who were willing in those days to carry disagreement with him to active lengths. So the Select Committee set to work, and in the following October reported the results of its deliberations, together with plans drawn up by the eminent Sir Giles Gilbert Scott, for a new chamber on the same site as the old, and as like the old chamber in all its features as was compatible with modern ideas of ventilation and acoustics.[1] After some debate the report and the plans were adopted by the House, and since then the new chamber has been completed.

The decision to rebuild in a style so close to the old is deeply characteristic of the House of Commons. It exemplifies to the full that resolute grasp of tradition which attracted the attention of Carlyle in the passage quoted above. And as a matter of fact it conformed to an earlier decision which was very much in point.

The old House itself was, though to a lesser extent, made to resemble that earlier chamber which perished in the fire of 1834. This consisted of the walls and roof of the fourteenth-century Chapel of St Stephen, with a false ceiling, wooden panelling, and a gallery installed by Sir Christopher Wren in the reign of Queen Anne. But though the beautiful fenestration and paintings of the Plantagenet chapel were concealed by the classical embellishments of Wren, the chamber continued to bear the rectangular shape with which King Edward's architect endowed it; the seating ran lengthwise down the room, just as the stalls had run in the old chapel; and, where the altar had been, stood a fine canopied chair for Mr Speaker.

1. Acoustic considerations were not allowed to weigh too heavily against the force of aesthetics and tradition. The ceiling, for instance, was to be sloping, as before, though it was known that a ceiling of this shape reflected the sound waves.

The arrangements which were thus probably fortuitous in the earlier building were adopted deliberately in the chamber which was completed in 1852, against the wishes of the architect, who contemplated a large square room, capable of seating all the Members of the (then very large) House together. Barry's chamber was, in fact, substantially larger than St Stephen's Chapel: the classical moulding and Ionic pillars of Wren were supplanted by Gothic corbels and arches – a tribute to the popular Gothic revival then at its zenith – and a profusion of carving designed by Pugin took the place of the Grinling Gibbons of the earlier chamber. But the plan was the same: rectangular, with seats running lengthwise down the room, and the Speaker's chair at the head: and it is still the same. Even the temporary Houses (in Church House and the old House of Lords) were fitted out as far as possible to resemble exactly the old House of Commons. In fact, as Mr Churchill pointed out when the Committee was appointed, it would be difficult to see how our procedure could function if the shape of the chamber were altered. It has taken seven years to build a new chamber: it has taken five hundred years to evolve our procedure.

Let us try to conjure up a picture of the old chamber as it was before that fateful night in 1941 carried away a room of such glorious memories and such dreary ornamentation. It was not especially large – 68 feet by 45 feet at ground floor level; tiny in comparison with the dim perspectives of the Hall of Representatives at Washington (93 feet by 139 feet). It had a cosy appearance which was enhanced by the deep overhanging galleries all round the room, and by the fact that all the available floor space was packed with seating of the traditional pew-like variety. It was essentially a chamber which lent itself to close debate, repartee, intervention, rejoinder, rather than sounding rhetoric. There was no tribune; and experience showed that the consequent necessity of speaking from a bench half-way up the House (the benches rose in tiers on either side) made rolling periods and rousing invective extremely difficult. Oratory to any extent was possible only from the front bench, particularly from the despatch-boxes – of which more anon.[1]

There can be no doubt that the smallness and intimacy[2] of the old chamber, continuing the tradition of the even smaller and more intimate Wren chamber, have had a very far-reaching effect upon English political life and feeling. They have probably contributed towards the comparative moderation and willingness to compromise which are characteristic of British politics. And it has certainly been responsible for maintaining the reality and life of the proceedings in the chamber, and for preventing them from becoming a mere echo of subterraneous intrigues or a repetition of discussions in cabal and committee.[3]

1. With this difficulty in mind, one Member even suggested to the Select Committee on Rebuilding that a tall brass rail should be placed upon the backs of the benches of the new chamber, so that the speakers could be ensured of its friendly support when faint with the birth-pangs of a new philippic: but this does not appear to have been adopted in the Committee's report.

2. The friendly, intimate atmosphere of the old House was never a feature of the House of Lords, even when converted to a temporary House of Commons. The greater area and height of the chamber, and the narrowness of the galleries, were doubtless responsible for this. Perhaps also the intention of the designer had something to do with it. The Lords' chamber was the place where Pugin really 'let himself go'. It has something of real, though faded, magnificence.

3. The old chamber provided seats for only 346 of a 1941 total membership of 615; and the dimensions and seating arrangements for Members of the new chamber are the same as those of the old (346 for 624). Much controversy has raged over this decision: but it was practically dictated to the Select Committee by the leaders of the majority party in the House. Mr Churchill, when introducing the subject of the new chamber in the House, alluded to the numerous advantages of debating in a small chamber, and the depressing effect of meeting in a large

Whether, however, the seating arrangements of the physical House can be held responsible for the development of the English two-party system, as Mr Churchill seemed to allege on a famous occasion,[1] is a matter of more doubt. It is true that the separation of the longitudinal benches into two groups, left and right, would seem to favour a strictly dual division of membership. Yet there were, in the old chamber, and are in the new chamber, at the end furthest from the Speaker, cross-benches, which, though technically 'outside the House', are yet used by Members listening to the debates. Whenever a party has a large majority in the House (i.e. more often than not) some Members of the majority, sometimes a large part of the majority, have to seep across into the left-hand benches. And, after all, nowhere is the two-party system more rigidly developed than in the American House of Representatives, where the seating is arranged in a semicircle.

In any visit to the House of Commons either before the destruction of the old chamber, or since the opening of the new chamber, our gaze would naturally be attracted, should the House be in Session, to the canopied chair at the head of the chamber, where Mr Speaker sits in the traditional dress of knee-breeches and long black gown – perhaps in the traditional posture, head resting on his hand, both enveloped in the curls of a full-bottomed wig. Beneath him, at a long, rectangular table, at the Table of the House, the three Clerks, also in wig and gown, sit recording the decisions of the House. On this table, but on opposite sides

chamber that is half-empty. Despite all the advantages of modern amplification, close debate is practically impossible in a room much larger than the old House. The present writer recalls with some unhappiness a visit to a meeting of UNO in a large hall in London. The House of Commons is sometimes dull, but it can never be as dull as that!

1. The debate on rebuilding (see *Hansard*, 393 H.C. Deb. 5s. col. 404).

near the end furthest from Mr Speaker, always rest two despatch-boxes, bound in brass filagree:[1] and at the end of the table is the glittering mace, the symbol of the King's authority, resting on two hooks. At the other end of the chamber, in one of the shorter cross-benches, is a chair for the Serjeant at Arms. He also appears in black knee-breeches, but, unlike Mr Speaker, is girt with a sword, and sits bare-headed. On the green leather-covered benches on either side sit or lounge the representatives of the people, occasionally in large numbers, as on the occasion of some crucial speech, but more often in ones or twos, like scattered oases in a vast desert of green leather. On the front bench upon the Speaker's right sit the principal Members of the Government: ministers, under-secretaries, and whips. On the opposite front bench sit the leaders of the Opposition, and other privy councillors. These benches are known as the Treasury bench and the Opposition front bench respectively. Front-bench Members have the privilege of anchoring themselves to the despatch-boxes on the table while delivering their speeches, so that they can clutch, smite, and lean upon them. Mr Gladstone's signet rings did almost as much damage to the old despatch-boxes, through a parliamentary life of half a century, as his oratory did to the cause of Protection and the Ottoman Empire. Indeed he is said to have showered blows upon the box and the table, and even on one occasion to have struck the mace itself.[2]

Round the green benches of the old chamber clustered many famous memories, of great events, and of great personages. There so often Gladstone, with his white hair and flashing eyes, had leant upon the table and pointed his finger at

1. The old famous black boxes were destroyed in the bombing. The elaborate new boxes, of an exotic ruby wood, were a gift from the Dominion of New Zealand.

2. Earl Curzon of Kedleston, *Modern Parliamentary Eloquence*, p. 27.

his great opponent sitting opposite him – Disraeli, immovable, with arms folded, and inscrutable dark eyes fixed on the ground. Those two figures, with their words and their actions, seem to sum up the history of England – nay, of the whole world – in the nineteenth century. The ghosts of Parnell and the Irish obstructionists – the huge figure of Bradlaugh – the bearded visage of the elder Churchill[1] – the elegant Joseph Chamberlain – a hundred figures that are part of history, and, in a manner, part of ourselves, lingered amid the dim oaken woodwork of that old chamber. Palmerston, straight as a die (though over seventy years of age) had sat there with his hat over his eyes throughout the whole of many a long parliamentary day, and pretended to slumber; Lord John Russell had sat there, leaning backwards, with his arms folded across his chest; Balfour, sitting on his shoulder-blades, and contemplating the glass ceiling with philosophic detachment. Great speeches had thundered across the floor – Gladstone on the Bulgarian atrocities in 1877, for instance, a speech which Balfour afterwards said would always be unequalled 'as a feat of parliamentary courage, parliamentary skill, parliamentary endurance, and parliamentary eloquence'; Asquith, 'the last of the Romans', denouncing Tariff Reform; and last and certainly not least the younger Churchill avowing the intention of the nation, in the last extremity of peril, so to bear itself that if the British Empire were to endure a thousand years, 'men will still say, "this was their finest hour".'

A few months after this speech was delivered the chamber which re-echoed to the delighted cheering of his hearers was destroyed. Almost all the arrangements and topography of

1. It has been suggested to me that the beard was not characteristic of Lord Randolph Churchill in his prime. But he certainly appeared in the chamber with a beard in 1893 – see for example the illustration in Lucy's *Peeps at Parliament*, p. 63.

the old chamber have been reproduced in the new. There are a few improvements. The accommodation for visitors is increased by 137 seats; the interior decoration is more restrained; the wood-carving is less indiscriminately exuberant; the grim, varnished woodwork of old has been replaced by a more modern, and, it is hoped, slightly less depressing grey oak, and a new system of ventilation[1] prescribed by Dr Oscar Faber replaces the old method of pumping dry, smelly air through the floor. Some of these improvements have been slightly disappointing: the fluorescent lighting is a curious pink, and the acoustics, even with amplifiers, are not perfect. Members at the bar, or behind the Chair, often cannot hear the front bench speakers (this deficiency in acoustics has been attributed to the greater restraint in ornament: Pugin's extensive carving in some way helped the sound). The new chamber is perhaps a more comfortable place; but it hardly retains the memories of the old chamber, and it is unlikely that it will, in the end, prove the scene of events such as the old chamber witnessed.

> The oldest hath borne most; we that are young
> Shall never see so much, nor live so long.

Something must be said of the Palace of Westminster, of which the House of Commons forms a part. This huge range of neo-Gothic buildings, with its fine towers, which lines the Thames at Westminster, is the most outstanding instance of how near the modern architect may approach the Gothic ideal, and how impossible it is for him to attain it. The architect, Sir Charles Barry, was not, as a matter of fact, a Gothic architect by conviction. Perhaps it is for that reason that the river front of the Palace is so lovely, as seen from a distance, from the other side of the river, for instance, and

1. By alternating streams of fresh air, cleaned and heated by electric plates.

so uninteresting when examined at close quarters. Barry had all the fine sense of proportion and outline of a Renaissance architect; and only on the river front had he a real opportunity to exercise his talents. But his junior collaborator, Pugin, was an almost fanatical admirer of the Gothic style. All the interior decoration, and much of the exterior detail is his work. And it is the sort of work which compels admiration rather than deep pleasure.

Although the Palace of Westminster, as rebuilt by Barry, covers eight acres of ground, and contains eleven hundred rooms, there has never been anything like adequate accommodation for Members. They have a spacious library, smoking-room, and refreshment rooms: somewhat less spacious dining-rooms for guests. Before 1950 they had only two miles of corridor in which to talk to their friends and dictate their letters to their secretaries. They each have a little locker in which to keep a few papers. Only Ministers, and Chairmen of important Committees, have rooms of their own. It was, however, discovered that in the space which Barry used for the old chamber, several floors and a number of extra rooms could be built. It would appear that the greater part of the total volume of the old chamber and its appurtenances was only ventilating space which had not even efficiency to recommend it. Hence, in the dim recesses under the new chamber there have been installed conference rooms, interviewing rooms, and small secretarial rooms:[1] while above it there are offices for the staff of the House of Commons, and the 'pool' of Members' secretaries and typists.

Something has therefore been done to provide greater facilities for the work and comfort of Members. But the average M.P. must still expect to lead a rather uncomfort-

1. Since this was written a house has been fitted out for Members' secretaries in Old Palace Yard, just opposite the Palace.

able existence when attending upon his parliamentary
duties. He must expect to spend many boring and frustrated hours in the chamber. He will spend his time out of
the chamber either in the library, dealing with his correspondence, in the refreshment rooms, taking his meals, in
the smoking-room, sharing his feelings with his colleagues,
in the depths of the earth dictating letters to a typist, or – if
he can afford it – in the rooms of the various secretarial
agencies which are available for Members within the
Palace. There are no other amenities except the river
Terrace, radio and television sets, and an occasional cinematograph show. In spite of all this, he will probably find
great enjoyment in his parliamentary life. What rooms are
available to him in the Palace are extremely spacious and
comfortable. The whole of the building has a dignity which
modern erections, because of their economy and efficiency,
are unable to achieve. Members felt this deeply when, in
consequence of bombing, they were forced to move into the
neighbouring Church House, an almost brand-new building, in 1940,[1] 1941 and 1944.

This, briefly, is the setting of the parliamentary drama.
We may now pass on to consider the character and the rules
of the play.

1. In November 1940 Parliament was actually opened by the King
in Church House.

CHAPTER II

THE BASIS OF PROCEDURE

LET us begin by asking ourselves what purpose procedure serves. The superficial answer, of course, will tend to vary. Members of the Opposition will tend to hold that the purpose of procedure is to prevent the Government from exercising autocratic power, in short to prevent it from doing what it likes. The cabinet minister will tend to say that procedure is designed to prevent the Opposition from talking too much: i.e. from obstructing business. And indirectly, of course, there is some truth in this. But essentially, surely, the purpose of procedure is to enable the will or the opinion of an assembly to be focused and clearly expressed. This, we must remember, is theory, whereas procedure is a matter of practice. We shall find, later on, that theory and practice can be sometimes curiously at variance.

If we bear this central purpose in mind, we shall more easily grasp the reason for the various basic forms which are the alphabet of parliamentary business. We shall not, of course, be able to say in every case, or indeed in most cases, why a certain form or formula is used. As Hatsell, the great Clerk of the House of the eighteenth century, has expressed it: 'In these instances, and in every other of this sort, it is more material that there should be a rule to go by, than what that rule is: in order that there may be a uniformity of proceeding in the business of the House, not subject to the momentary caprice of the Speaker, or to the captious disputes of any of the Members. If the maxim, "Stare super vias antiquas" has ever any weight, it is in these matters, where it is not so material, that the rule should be established on the foundation of sound reason and argument, as it is, that order, decency, and regularity, should be preserved in a large, a numerous, and consequently sometimes tumultuous assembly.'

Broadly speaking, then, the will of the House of Commons is expressed in *orders*, and its opinions in the form of *resolutions*.[1] But it should be remembered that the House usually gives *orders* only to its own servants – the officials of the House, the police on duty in the precincts of the Palace and the approaches thereto, and the Committees chosen from the House. Outside this rather limited field it has no executive authority. The House of Commons cannot order the army to invade Heligoland – only the King, acting on the advice of his ministers, can do that. It cannot close all cinemas on Sunday: only the whole legislative authority can do that – i.e. King, Lords and Commons acting together.[2] If the House of Commons wishes to impose its will outside its own rooms it must do so by legislation. In other words it must pass a *Bill*, which will become law only when it has also received the assent of the King and the Lords.

Motions

All resolutions and orders begin as *motions*:[3] and every Bill proceeds by a series of motions. Everyone knows what a

1. There is one exception to this general rule. The House cannot give orders to itself; its will as regards its own actions is expressed in resolutions. It should also be noted that the House has powers to summon outsiders to attend it as witnesses, etc., and to require the assistance of public officers such as magistrates.

2. But in this as in other matters the Executive (i.e. the Government) has now been given powers to act sometimes alone, by making Orders, Rules, Statutory Instruments, etc.

3. Motions which are to become resolutions are sometimes loosely referred to as 'resolutions'. Thus Mr Gladstone is said to have moved a series of *resolutions* on Irish Church Disestablishment, in 1868.

motion looks like. Here is one that was proposed (but not carried) on 3 June 1803, when war with Napoleon had broken out afresh:

That it was the duty of His Majesty's Ministers to make timely and adequate representations against such acts as have, in their judgement, constituted a series of aggression, violence, and insult, on the part of *France:* That, by dignified and temperate remonstrances, followed up with consistency, and sustained with firmness, either the course and progress of such acts would have been arrested, without the necessity of recurring to Arms, or the determination of the *French* Government to persist therein, would have been distinctly ascertained, before His Majesty had, by the reduction of His forces, and the surrender of His conquests, put out of His hands the most effectual means of obtaining redress and reparation: That this essential duty appears to have been, in a very great degree, neglected by His Majesty's Ministers; and that such their neglect and omission have been highly injurious to the public interests.

And here, as a contrast, is a motion which was proposed (and carried) a hundred and forty-two years later, on 8 May 1945:

That this House do now attend at the church of St Margaret, Westminster, to give humble and reverent thanks to Almighty God for our deliverance from the threat of German domination.

A motion is simply an expression of the opinion or the wish of one Member of the House, which he puts before the House so that, if the House votes for it, it will become the opinion or the will of the whole assembly. A unanimous vote is hard to come by in an assembly of 625 Members; and for that reason a *majority assent* to a motion is accepted in lieu of unanimity. In other words, if more than half of the Members who vote vote for the motion, it is carried.

Now obviously a Member cannot get up at any time and move any motion that he likes. The exigencies of time make that impossible. The Government, which to a large extent controls the programme of the House, must see to it that its business is dealt with first; and any other motions have to wait for an opportunity, which may never arise.

So the right to move a motion is closely restricted. But any Member can 'put down' a motion: all he has to do is to write it on a scrap of paper and hand it in to the Clerks at the Table. It will then be printed in the Order Paper. If an opportunity is given to discuss it it will be moved, seconded, and debated. Eventually the House will vote upon it, and if a majority of the Members present vote in favour of it, it will become an expression of the views of the whole assembly.

Motions are put down for all kinds of reasons. They are put down by the leaders of the Government, by the leaders of the Opposition, and by Private Members, though motions set down by the latter have normally little chance of being debated, much less of being carried. Private Members' motions in fact are frequently not intended to be debated. They are usually set down 'for an early day'; and printed on the Order Paper under the heading 'Notices of Motions for which no day has been fixed.'[1] No one actually expects them to come before the House on 'an early day', or even to come before the House at all. They are put down to give advertisement and expression to the opinions which they embody, so that by this means other Members, and possibly even the Government, may be influenced in the direction of those opinions. Thus, for instance, in a recent Parliament a motion was put down by a Private Member censuring the conduct of the Allies in supporting Admiral Darlan. It remained on the Order Book long after Darlan had been shot and forgotten, since no one could take it off but the Member responsible. Similarly, some rather odd motions were put down by a certain Member who chose this method of ex-

1. Until a motion is actually moved it is, strictly speaking, only a *notice of motion*.

pressing his deep-seated aversion for the Jews. No attention was paid to them or expected to be paid to them by the House. By the end of one Session sixty-four motions stood upon the Order Book, ranging in subject from 'Married Women in the Civil Service' to 'Increase of Goat Stocks'.

Some opportunity, however, is always given to Private Members to move their motions. Up to the outbreak of war arrangements were made for the discussion of Private Members' motions on certain Wednesdays up to Easter. With the outbreak of war the Government appropriated all Private Members' time for its own Bills and the other business essential for the prosecution of the war; and the Labour Government decided to continue this arrangement during the reconstruction period; so that from 1939 until after the end of the war there were very few motions debated which were not Government motions: but the pre-war Private Member's time has now been largely restored to him. The subject of Private Members' time will be more fully dealt with in Chapter III. Usually the leaders of the Opposition, too, are given time to move one or two of their own motions in a Session.

Moving and Seconding

When the time comes the Member who is called upon will move his motion with a speech, or simply with the words 'I beg to move'.[1] If it is an Order of the Day he can make a formal gesture, and save up his speech until later, so that he can reply to criticism. Generally speaking, a Member must move his own motion, and if he expects that he will be unable to be present at the appointed time he must ask another Member to add his name to the motion on the Order Paper:

1. If the motion is printed on the Order Paper, he need not repeat it to the House.

the motion is then the other Member's motion too, and he can move it for him. For the purpose of motions, however, Members of the Government are interchangeable: motions moved by Members of the Government or the Privy Council need no seconder. Orders of the day (the items of business set down on the order paper for consideration that day) need no seconder either, and the same is true of motions to proceed with stages of Bills ('ancillary motions'); but these two sorts of motion are in any case usually Government motions. In other cases, if no one will rise to second the motion, it lapses, and the next item of business is called.

An instance of this occurred in the case of the London, Midland and Scottish Railway Bills, on 14 December 1944. On that occasion the Member for Worcester, after delivering a rousing speech on behalf of his motion against them, was unable to find a seconder; and after a moment Mr Speaker declared his motion to have lapsed. No debate could then take place, and as it happened, the Member for Worcester had made pointed references to another Member, to which the other Member was thus unable to reply. His only remedy would have been to second his attacker's motion himself.

The Question

After the seconder has spoken Mr Speaker rises and *proposes* the question[1] thus: '*The question is* that this House regrets that, instead of making the burden of unemployment a national charge, His Majesty's Government have driven large numbers of able-bodied unemployed persons to seek

1. Readers will, of course, distinguish between 'the question' and parliamentary questions to ministers (see p. 104 ff.). In earlier days it was the duty of the Speaker to frame a question himself from the general drift of the mover's remarks. He then 'proposed' the question for general debate. See Scobell, *Memorials of the Method and Manner of Proceedings in Parliament.*

the aid of the Poor Law, thereby exhausting the resources of an ever-increasing number of local authorities'[1] (or whatever are the exact terms of the motion).

At the end of the debate the Speaker *puts* the question. He repeats exactly what he said when proposing the question, and adds, 'As many as are of that opinion say "aye": as many as are of the contrary opinion say "no".' He must then make an estimate of the respective weight of the voices, and say, 'I think the "ayes" have it', or 'I think the "noes" have it' accordingly. If there are still answering cries of the opposite opinion he must call out 'Clear the lobbies!', and the House *divides*. The machinery of a division is described in a later section (p. 113 ff.).

Members may speak at any time from the proposing of the question until the voices for the negative have been given. The length of the debate is usually settled by the various party whips beforehand. There are, of course, occasions when the party will not 'come to heel'. But usually the general desire to get it over and go home prevails, and as soon as the Government spokesman has answered the debate the Speaker puts the question.

Resolutions and Orders

The motion, if carried, usually becomes a *Resolution*, and is entered in the minutes of the House accordingly.

Resolved, That it appears to this House, That *Robert* Lord *Clive*, Baron of *Plassey*, in the Kingdom of *Ireland*, about the Time of the deposing of *Surajah Dowlah*, Nabob of *Bengal*, and the establishing of *Meer Jaffier* on the Musnud, did obtain and possess himself of Two Lacks and 80,000 Rupees, as Member of the Select Committee; a further Sum of Two Lacks of Rupees as Commander in Chief; and a further Sum of 16 Lacks of Rupees, or more, under the Denomination of private Donation; which Sums, amounting

1. 12 April 1933.

together to 20 Lacks, and 80,000 Rupees, were of the Value in *English* Money, of £234,000.[1]

Resolved, That this House welcomes the intention of His Majesty's Government, declared in the White Paper presented to Parliament, to introduce measures for the conservation and better utilization of the country's water resources, the improvement of the administration of water supply, the further extension of public water supplies and sewerage in rural localities and the better management of rivers.[2]

The motion may, as already mentioned, take the form of an order. Thus, after the visit of King Charles I, and his attempt to seize the five Members, we find this entry in the Journals:

Ordered, That another Locke be set upon the Door under the Stairs, at the Doore of the Commons House and that Mr *Bell* keep the Key, and search it every morning.[3]

Sometimes the debate on a motion is not even taken as far as 'putting the question'. Once the question has been *proposed*, however, the motion is no longer in the hands of the mover: it can be withdrawn only by the general consent of the House. If, after debate, the Member responsible for the motion feels satisfied with the Government's answer to his point, or if he feels that the subject has already been sufficiently ventilated, he will rise and beg leave to withdraw the motion. The Speaker will thereupon say 'Is it your pleasure that the motion be withdrawn' and then – without giving too much time for the irresponsibles to say 'no' – 'Motion by leave withdrawn'. Occasions have occurred where motions have very nearly been put to the vote, to the great embarrassment of the mover, because some Member insisted upon speaking to the motion after the mover had signified his intention to withdraw.

1. 21 May 1773.   2. 4 May 1944.   3. January 1641.

Frequently motions come before the House on which no one has anything to say. In fact there are a number of motions which by Standing Order must be settled at once, without debate. In such cases the Speaker will put the question as soon as the motion is moved, and it will be decided forthwith. The most important of these is the motion to suspend the rule by which the House rises at 10.30 p.m., which is discussed in a later chapter (see p. 53). The reason for forbidding debate in this case is, of course, that the motion is purely a matter of machinery, and that the House ought not to be allowed to spend time debating whether to allow itself more time to debate: it is a matter for speedy decision.

The Adjournment

To the average layman it will be plain that it is of the utmost importance that the motions proposed to the House should be clear, concise and meaningful. They must be capable of expressing the opinion or the will of the assembly when they are voted upon. They must be capable of being closely debated. 'There can be no vote and no decision,' says Redlich, 'without a precisely framed question.' And yet, this is just what is not the case with a large proportion of the motions debated in the House of Commons. The motion which is debated more frequently than anything else is 'that this House do now adjourn', and in a great number of cases the mover would be extremely embarrassed if this motion was carried, and the House did adjourn. Frequently the motion is withdrawn, or negatived, or killed by the 'hour of interruption' – the automatic interruption of business at 10.0. And the debates on it have normally nothing whatever to do with the advisability or otherwise of adjourning. They are concerned with all kinds of topics. *The adjournment*, as it is called, is simply a peg to hang them on.

The great debate which took place in the House of Commons upon 7 and 8 May 1940, which resulted in the resignation of Mr Chamberlain's Government and the succession of Mr Churchill as Prime Minister, was certainly one of the crucial moments of the last war. After two days' passionate and, at times, acrimonious debate a vote was taken, and though the result showed a majority for the Government, it was so small a majority, in comparison with the relative strength of the party, that the Prime Minister considered it was his duty to resign. This was a debate in the grand style. It had a flavour reminiscent of those great debates of Napoleonic times which we all read about in our history books at school. The shadow of Pitt and Fox hung over the assembly. Yet the reader will be very disappointed if he searches the *Votes and Proceedings*[1] or the *Journals* of the House for a record of the great occasion. All that he will find is this:

Adjournment, – Motion made, and Question put, 'That this House do now adjourn:' – (*Captain Margesson*) – the House *divided;* Ayes 281, Noes 200.

Two days' debate, two hundred and thirty columns of *Hansard*, a Government overthrown, complacency shaken to its foundations – and the House resolves to adjourn at its usual time. The motion seems strangely unsuited to the issues involved.

By way of contrast, let us turn back in the *Journals* to a similar occasion during the Napoleonic wars. On 23 and 24 May 1803, in the course of a debate on the war situation, Pitt delivered one of the greatest speeches of his career, and Charles James Fox (who spoke from ten o'clock until one o'clock in the morning) delivered a speech, says Mr Speaker Abbott, 'of more art, eloquence, wit and mischief than I remember to have heard from him.' But the motion upon

1. See below, p. 122

which this great debate turned was a very different affair from that of 8 May 1940. It was in the form of an amendment to the Address to the King, and ran as follows:

To leave out from the word 'commands', at the end of the first paragraph, to the end of the Question, in order to insert these words; 'To assure His Majesty of our firm determination to co-operate with His Majesty in calling forth the resources of the United Kingdom, for the vigorous prosecution of the War in which we are involved, and to express to His Majesty the satisfaction with which His faithful Commons have received His Majesty's gracious Declaration, that he is willing to afford, as far as may be consistent with His own honour and the interests of His People, every facility to any just arrangement, by which the blessings of Peace may be restored to His loyal Subjects.'

The curious convention by which a Member 'moves the adjournment of the House' in order to discuss a matter of importance is an interesting example of the way in which the House instinctively adapts an old custom to new and strange uses. There are three distinct stages in its development. There is (1) the original, obvious use of the motion 'that this House do now adjourn' in order to end the sitting, so that Members can go home. Right up to 1888, as we shall see, the House could be adjourned only by a motion, and, on occasion, Members have left the Speaker stranded in the Chair. In 1888 a system of adjourning the House without question put was introduced, but even after that the House could be adjourned only with Mr Speaker in the chair, unless his unavoidable absence has previously been announced, so that although he might give place to his deputy and retire to bed when the debate seemed likely to last into the small hours, he had to get up and come down to the House again, no matter at what time, simply to say 'This House now stands adjourned'. It has since been arranged that the Deputy Speaker or his deputy may adjourn the House in place of the Speaker. It should be understood that the House can still be adjourned by motion, and in fact frequently is.

Then there is (2) the use of the motion to interfere with or hold up the business of the House, a habit which has given it the name of 'dilatory motion'. Thus a Member rises to move the adjournment, not at the end of a sitting, but in the middle of a debate.[1] We hear a good deal of this practice towards the end of the eighteenth century, in the time of Burke and Pitt. James Grant records that one night Sheridan moved the adjournment nineteen successive times, to prevent the House passing a resolution to which he was opposed; and that the House at length gave it up in disgust, and allowed the adjournment to be carried. At a later period Speaker Denison records[2] that a small but persistent minority moved the adjournment eight or nine times in the course of a single sitting on the Clergy Disabilities Bill (1870). They would have moved it even oftener, had he not ruled that a single Member could not move the adjournment more than once in the course of a debate on one motion, so that when each Member of the minority had moved his adjournment once, they were unable to hold up business any further. Nowadays the right to move the adjournment has been even more drastically curtailed by a Standing Order (No. 26)[3] by which the Speaker can refuse to accept a motion for the adjournment of the House if he thinks it is an abuse of the rules of the House – which means that persistent obstruc-

1. Hatsell tells us that the first instance of this occurred in 1677, so that it is not old as parliamentary customs go.

2. p. 259.

3. The Standing Orders of the House of Commons are published by H.M. Stationery Office (price 6/6) and are reprinted at frequent intervals. There are 112 Standing Orders relative to public business, and 249 Standing Orders relative to private business – for which see Chapter VII.

tion by adjournment motions is now impossible. It is now accepted (though this is not expressly stated in the Standing Orders) that between separate Orders of the Day only a Member of the Government can move the adjournment.

There is (3) the use of the adjournment to allow Members to talk about something other than the subject of the motion then before the House. From the earliest times, if a Member spoke away from the point, the Speaker would interfere: but the question of adjourning or not adjourning obviously has wide implications, and it became an accepted convention that on such motions it was in order to talk about anything under the sun. For instance the famous long sitting of 1881, which will be referred to in the next chapter, was mostly occupied by motions for the adjournment introduced into the debate on the Bill which was before the House. On these motions the speeches roamed over very wide fields indeed, though the Speaker frequently interposed and attempted to bring the Member back to the question of adjourning. (He had in those days no power to order a Member to desist from speaking.) Similarly if some matter arose which aroused debate immediately – for instance a personal statement by a Member – it was the practice to move the adjournment, so that there would be at any rate some motion before the House. Here is an instance. The news of the disastrous defeat of Lord Chelmsford by the Zulus at Isandlwana reached England in March 1879. On 15 March, a Member took the opportunity at question-time of asking the Government whether they intended to place the supreme command in South Africa 'in other hands'. Sir Stafford Northcote replied that 'as at present advised they are not prepared to adopt this course.' The Member then immediately moved the adjournment of the House and a stormy debate ensued.

This practice also has been severely restricted in recent times. The use of the adjournment as a motion for general debate is now confined (a) to the beginning of business[1] before any other motion has been moved, when it must be moved by a Member of the Government, and (b) to the special use of the adjournment under Standing Order No. 9, to discuss a 'definite matter of urgent public importance', which is explained in Chapter III (p. 65).

There is finally (4), the ingenious modern practice by which the Government, as a sort of concession to the Opposition and other Private Members, whose opportunities of criticism have been restricted by various curtailments of the power of moving the adjournment, moves the adjournment at the beginning of the day (= after question-time). In this way matters which are too general to be framed in the terms of a specific motion may be debated – for the House cannot debate unless there is some motion before it. What generally happens is that when representations are made to the Government whips and the leader of the House that debate on a certain subject is urgently desired, arrangements will be made for a Member of the Government to move the adjournment of the House on a day determined in advance, after question-time, and before the Orders of the Day are read. The debate will then begin on the subject previously determined upon and Members are able to speak on the whole matter, without having to pay regard to the wording of a carefully framed motion.

It has also been arranged to have the same sort of debate every evening during the last half-hour of the sitting. We shall have occasion to consider this arrangement later, when dealing with the hours of sitting (see p. 51).

The practice of having general debates upon adjournment motions is, in some ways, very useful. The House is able to come to a decision and vote on the matter, and, since

[1]. It is no longer in order to move the adjournment during question-time.

even if a vote is taken its opinion is not precisely expressed by it, the hands of the executive are unfettered by detailed instructions. On the other hand the practice of moving to adjourn the House in order to discuss a matter of the public welfare has its absurd side, whatever the precedents may be. It is both illogical and inconvenient. The lack of meaning in the resolution which is come to (if any resolution is come to) drastically reduces the control which the House claims to exercise over the executive. And it is sometimes difficult to know what exactly the vote on an adjournment motion means.

The following is a case in point. Members of Parliament are entitled to free copies of the daily (paper-backed) issue of *Hansard*. In 1943 a debate took place upon the question of whether bound volumes of *Hansard* should also be issued to them free of charge or not. The decision on the matter rested with the Speaker: but he felt obliged to follow the recommendations (a) of the Government, (b) of a Select Committee of the House, and (c) of the orders of the House itself, if it gave any. The Government were anxious to economize in paper: but they were also anxious to please the House. So they laid the onus of responsibility upon the Select Committee, which had strongly advised against issuing bound volumes free, in view of the war-time paper scarcity, and the general desirability of economy. The Government spokesman said that it was entirely a matter for the Select Committee. They were themselves, he said, willing to provide the money, the paper and the labour.

The debate took place upon a motion for the adjournment, moved by the Government. It became extremely heated, and the House divided. The result was a majority for the motion: but to this day no one quite knows what this division meant. The feeling of the House was clear from the speeches; Members wanted free bound volumes of *Hansard*;

but it was not clearly represented by the ensuing resolution.

The same principle, with its attendant advantages and disadvantages, governs all the voting of funds to the Government for the public services whether in the House or in Committee of the whole House. The motion may be 'that a sum not exceeding £241,926,000 be granted to His Majesty, on account, for or towards defraying the charges for Civil and Revenue Departments for the year ending on the 31st day of March 1945', but the debate may rage round the shape of the postmen's hats, or the wickedness of pampering the working classes. And there are other 'dilatory' motions, besides the adjournment of the House, which are used in the same way – e.g. 'That the debate be now adjourned', 'That the Chairman do report progress and ask leave to sit again.' Then there is another motion of a similar kind, formerly very frequently used, which has now quite dropped out of fashion, though it is still uncircumscribed by the restrictions which have been imposed upon the adjournment. This motion, which is known as the 'previous question'[1] consists of the formula 'that the question be not now put'. If the motion is *carried*, the question which was before the House when the 'previous question' was moved disappears. But if the motion is *negatived* the question which was previously before the House must be put immediately, because the House has in effect resolved that the question *be* now put. Hence the 'previous question' is still used in America as an equivalent to our *closure*[2] – of which more

1. The explanation of the name 'previous question' suggested by Redlich is that there is always a previous question to be settled before deciding any question – namely, whether the question should or should not be decided.

2. The form of it used in America is 'That the question be now put' – which was the form used in this country before 1888. The difference between this and closure (see below), is that a closure motion cannot be debated.

anon. Many of the great speeches of Pitt and Burke were made upon the 'previous question': the diary of Mr Speaker Abbott[1] is studded with it. Nowadays it is very rarely moved, and when, in 1943, Mr Hopkinson moved the 'previous question' in opposition to the motion to appoint a deputy chairman, he felt impelled to apologize for the novelty of the proceeding.[2]

Generally speaking most of the debating in the House takes place, not on a motion which will, when voted upon, express the will or opinion of the assembly in precise terms, but upon a motion which is quite unrelated to the subject of debate. The will of the assembly is 'gathered' from the tone of the speeches; and the Government shapes its plans accordingly: or, in the last resort, the assembly expresses its confidence or lack of confidence in the Government, with regard to this or that matter, by agreeing to or negativing the motion. And thus does practice differ from any theory which a writer might rashly preface to a work upon procedure.

Amendments

The House may express its opinion by agreeing to a motion, or by negativing it. There is a third possibility. The House may alter the motion, by agreeing to an *amendment* to it.

Any Member can put forward an amendment at any stage of a debate. In practice, however, it is usual to give notice beforehand, by writing the amendment out, and handing it in to the Clerks at the Table, so that it appears on the Order Paper next day. It is particularly advisable to do this, since Mr Speaker has power, by a process known as

1. Speaker 1802–17.
2. The 'previous question' may not be moved in committee, on an amendment, or upon a 'business' motion. In 1943 it had not been moved for 32 years.

'kangaroo'[1] to ignore amendments; to select only the amendments which he thinks are representative of important sections of opinion; and he will almost certainly refuse an amendment of which notice has not been given.

In debating amendments, the House of Commons follows a more precise and logical method than the method which is customary in meetings of clubs and societies outside. The layman will find it rather technical at first, but a little study of it will certainly convince him of its superiority.

First of all, then, we divide all amendments into three classes:

(a) Amendments to alter the motion by leaving out certain words;
(b) Amendments to alter the motion by adding or inserting certain words;
(c) Amendments to alter the motion by leaving out certain words and adding or inserting others.

In the House of Commons it is customary, not to debate an amendment as if it were an altogether separate question, but to debate it in relation to the motion which it affects. In each case the amendment is phrased to the effect that words should be (a) left out of, (b) added to, or inserted in, or (c) left out and added to or inserted in the original motion: and the question proposed on the amendment follows in the same style.

The amendment is moved and seconded just like any other motion. When Mr Speaker rises to propose the question on the amendment he will begin by saying, in the case of type (a):

'The original question was that [the terms of the original motion]; since when an amendment has been proposed to

1. Because the House 'hops over' intervening amendments on the Order Paper. This power was conferred in 1909.

leave out all the words from (say) "moreover" to "whereas".'

Type (b) would be proposed in the same way, except that Mr Speaker would say: 'Since when an amendment has been proposed in line 6, after "beer" to *insert* (or add) "and all other intoxicating or otherwise malignant beverages".'

In the case of type (c) he would say: 'Since when an amendment has been proposed to *leave out* all the words from "pamper" to the end of the question *and add*, "persons engaged in manual and lower-clerical occupations".'

The Speaker will go on to say, in the case of type (a) (leaving out words): 'The question I have to propose is that the words proposed to be left out *stand part* of the question.'

'Now why,' the reader may ask, 'does not the Speaker propose the question simply thus, "that those words be left out"?' Such problems will frequently arise in the course of our study of procedure. It is an old custom, and, once again, the reader must be reminded that the House of Commons is very reluctant to relinquish its old habits. It has been repeatedly found that it is dangerous to introduce procedural changes without exceptionally good reason, that such changes generally have unexpected effects, and that the present condition of things conceals many remarkable advantages behind an occasional appearance of idiosyncrasy.

In this particular case it is possible to conceive of several reasons for putting the question upside down on a motion to leave out words. In the first place it allows the supporters of the original motion to vote in the affirmative in the crucial division. (This will become clearer later.) In the second place, if the House orders the words to be left out to stand part of the question, it means that they remain in the question *as they are:* and this prevents further amendments being offered to those particular words. But the real reason is probably historical. Scobell informs us that it was the custom in the early seventeenth century for the Speaker to formulate a question himself for general debate. If a Member had some point which he wanted to include in the question, a formal question was put, that those words 'stand part of the question'. If the general trend of the subsequent debate ran counter to the sense of part of the question, the part of the question which was disliked could be dropped out by general consent, and without any formal motion to that effect. If, however, any Member rose and indicated disagreement with the general opinion on this point, a formal question had to be put, that such-and-such words *stand part of the question*, before the main question was put. The modern practice follows this exactly, except that the motion to leave out is put formally, whereas in the old practice it was assumed.

Whether these reasons are sufficient to compensate for the confusion which is caused, even in the minds of old Members of Parliament, by this rather topsy-turvy way of putting the question is another matter entirely. It has been suggested that it might be a good plan to adopt the Australian method of proposing the question 'that the words proposed to be left out be left out.'[1]

The case of type (b) (adding or inserting words) is quite simple. The Speaker will just go on to say: 'The question I have to propose is that those words be there inserted (or added).'

In the case of type (c) an additional complication arises. The amendment has two sections, as it were – words are to be taken out, and words are to be put in; and so there are two consecutive questions: (1) 'That the words proposed to be left out stand part of the question', and (2) 'That those words be there added (or inserted).' In the House of Commons these two questions are proposed separately, and, if

---

1. *The Chairman's Handbook*, p. 78. Some convention, however, would then have to be adopted to prevent further amendment to the words ordered not to be left out: otherwise there might be much waste of time.

necessary, debated separately – unlike the normal practice outside the House, where the tendency is for an amendment of this kind to be debated as a solid entity.

It can hardly be denied that the parliamentary method is the better. The House might be agreeable to leaving out the words which the mover of the amendment proposes to delete: but it might wish to insert quite other words than those which he proposes to insert; and this method allows for variation if variation is desired. In short, it is more flexible, and therefore, in an assembly where so many different kinds of subject are debated, preferable.

After the amendment has been debated the Speaker must put the question; and he does this, as usual, by repeating almost exactly what he said when proposing the question, with the addition of the inquiry – 'Those of that opinion say "Aye" – of the contrary opinion say "No".'[1] It must be remembered that in the case of a type (a) amendment (to leave out words), if the question is *agreed to*, the amendment is *lost*, because the words which are proposed to be left out are ordered to 'stand part' of the question. If the question is *negatived* the amendment is *carried*, because the House has decided *not* to let those words stand part of the question. The case of a type (b) amendment (adding or inserting words) is more simple. If the question is carried, the amendment is carried.

The case of a type (c) amendment – to leave out words and put in others – is once again more complicated. Mr Speaker must first put the question, 'That the words proposed to be left out stand part of the question'. If this is decided in the affirmative there is, once again, an end of the amendment straight away, because it has not been decided to leave out any words, and it is therefore usually impossible to add or insert any more. But if it is decided in the negative,

1. This is a customary abbreviation.

he must proceed to put a second question: 'The question is, That those words be there added (or inserted).' If that is agreed to, the amendment is carried. But if it is negatived there will be a gap in the original motion. It will run thus: 'That this House welcomes the assurance of His Majesty's Government that men serving in the Forces – ' and then end abruptly:[1] or worse still, in a meaningless phrase such as: 'That a Select Committee be appointed to attend this House.' Another amendment will have to be proposed to fill the gap, or the original motion will have to be withdrawn or even negatived.[2]

It may help the reader at this point if he has a few examples before him.

Type (a) amendments are not a frequent occurrence. It is not usually easy to leave words out of a motion without suggesting any other words in substitution. But here is a case. On 6 May 1881, Mr Callan moved 'That in the opinion of this House it is expedient and necessary that measures should be taken in the present Session of Parliament to improve the conditions of Agricultural Labourers' Habitations in Ireland.'

The Liberal Government were at this time only lukewarm in their Irish sympathies: and so the Irish Secretary moved an amendment to leave out the words 'in the present Session of Parliament'.

The question proposed on this amendment was 'That the words "in the present Session of Parliament" stand part of

1. Erskine May relates the case of a question which, by this process, was reduced to the single word 'That'!

2. It should be remembered that once an amendment has been made to a motion no amendment can be offered to any part of it preceding the point at which the amendment has been made. Difficulties are sometimes caused by Members forgetting this, and attempting to amend part of a motion which has been passed. Their only remedy is to vote against the whole motion.

the question'. This question was put and negatived and so the amendment was carried. The motion itself was then put and carried. The Government was thus able to express a general sympathy with Mr Callan, but at the same time to avoid committing themselves to immediate action.

Here is a case of a type (b) amendment. On 25 January 1809, the Government moved 'That the thanks of this House be given to the Right Honourable Lieutenant General Sir Arthur Wellesley, Knight of the Most Honourable Order of the Bath, for the distinguished valour, ability, and conduct, displayed by him on 17 and 21 August last in *Portugal*, on the latter of which days he obtained at Vimiera over the Army of the Enemy a signal victory, honourable and glorious to British arms.'

It will be remembered that Wellesley, the future Duke of Wellington, had with him in this campaign an incompetent superior officer, who did little but frustrate his plans and prevent him from pressing home the advantages gained by his victory. The Opposition, however, were resolved to bring this 'dug-out' into the picture. So they moved an amendment to insert after the words 'given to', the words 'Lieutenant General Sir Harry Burrard, Knight of the Most Honourable Order of the Bath, for his meritorious conduct, and to – .' The question proposed on this amendment would have been 'That those words be there inserted', and if it had passed in the affirmative, the amendment would have been carried, and the gallant but stupid Burrard would have stood side by side with Wellington to receive the thanks of the House. Fortunately, however, the amendment was withdrawn. The main motion was then carried, and Wellesley was duly thanked by the Speaker.

An incident in the long and stormy history of Charles Bradlaugh's attempt to take his seat in the House will serve as an illustration of a type (c) amendment. Bradlaugh first attempted to take his seat in 1880. He was, as is well known, a professing atheist, and a combination of unlucky circumstances made his initial refusal to take the Oath prescribed by law into a sort of *cause célèbre*. It was not very well handled by the Speaker, and some of the younger Conservative Members (led by Lord Randolph Churchill) saw in it a glorious opportunity for embarrassing the Government. In spite of the fact that a Select Committee had reported against him, Bradlaugh made repeated attempts to sit in the House, to make Affirmation, even to administer the Oath to himself, only to find that every attempt was thwarted by Lord Randolph Churchill and his friends.

On 22 June 1880, Labouchere moved, 'That Mr Bradlaugh, Member for the Borough of Northampton, be admitted to make Affirmation or Declaration, instead of the Oath required by Law.'

By this time the more fanatical Members of the House had been thoroughly roused, and Sir Hardinge Gifford moved an amendment, to leave out all the words from 'That' to the end of the question, and add 'having regard to the Reports and proceedings of two Select Committees appointed by this House, Mr Bradlaugh be not permitted to take the Oath or make the Affirmation mentioned in the Statute 29 Vic. c. 19, and the Statute 31 and 32 Vic. c. 72.' The first question put was of course 'That the words proposed to be left out stand part of the Question.' This was negatived by a majority of forty-five. The next question put was 'That those words be there added.' This was also carried, and the *main question* was then put and carried, so that the final resolution was as follows:

Resolved, That, having regard to the Reports and proceedings of two Select Committees appointed by this House, Mr Bradlaugh be not permitted to take the Oath or make the Affirmation mentioned in the Statute 29 Vic. c. 19, and the 31 and 32 Vic. c. 72.

As a result of this decision the contest dragged on for years, with little honour either to the House or to the religion which was supposed to be involved in the point at issue. On one occasion Bradlaugh – a man of massive physique – was dragged out of the chamber by main force, and thrown into the street outside the Palace amid the cheers of his numerous adherents. It is said that the violence thus inflicted upon him was partly responsible for his early death. Eventually, when Arthur Peel had been elected to the Chair, Bradlaugh was allowed to take his seat without molestation, would-be protesters being firmly sat upon by the new and very strong-minded Speaker.

Sometimes amendments are proposed to amendments. It happened in December 1875 that orders were issued to the ships of the Navy that they were not to pick up or harbour slaves escaping (presumably by swimming) from the territories of slave-owning powers. On 22 February 1876 Mr Whitbread moved 'That in the opinion of this House, a Slave once admitted to the protection of the British Flag should be treated while on board one of Her Majesty's ships as if he were free, and should not be removed from or ordered to leave the ship on the ground of slavery.' To this the Government spokesman moved an amendment, to leave out from the word 'House' to the end of the Question, in order to add the words 'in order to maintain most effectually the right of personal liberty, it is desirable to await further information from the Report of a Royal Commission, both as to the instructions from time to time issued to British naval officers, the international obligations of this Country, and the attitude of other States in regard to the treatment of domestic Slaves on board of national ships.'

The question was then proposed 'That the words proposed to be left out stand part of the question,' and debated for the rest of that day, and most of a subsequent day. It was finally put and negatived by forty-five votes. The next question to be proposed was 'That the words "in order to maintain most effectually the right of personal liberty, it is desirable to await further information from the Report of a Royal Commission, both as to the instructions from time to time issued to British naval officers, the international obligations of this Country, and the attitude of other States in regard to the treatment of domestic Slaves on board of national ships" be there added.' At this stage Mr Fawcett moved an amendment after the word 'desirable' to insert 'provided that the Circular of the 5th day of December 1875 and the East Indies Station Order of 1871, on the subject of Fugitive Slaves, shall not continue in force' in the words proposed to be added.

The question 'That those words be there inserted' was accordingly put and negatived, again by forty-five votes. This left the original amendment as it stood. The question 'That the proposed words be there added' was then put and carried, and so the main question stood as follows:

That in the opinion of this House, in order to maintain most effectually the right of personal liberty, it is desirable to await further information from the Report of a Royal Commission, both as to the instructions from time to time issued to British naval officers, the international obligations of this Country, and the attitude of other States in regard to the treatment of domestic Slaves on board of national ships.

This was put and agreed to, without a division.

This is the case of a type (b) amendment to a type (c) amendment: but of course a great many combinations are possible in the way of amendments. One might even have an infinite series of amendments.

The reader will have realized that the process of voting upon a contentious motion may become very complicated.

In the case of a type (c) amendment, two questions have to be put on the amendment alone, before the motion itself can be put. But that is the least of it. There may be amendments to amendments; and there may be a 'closure' motion on each amendment. Closure is a refinement which must be fully explained in another section:[1] it is enough to say that it is the rule rather than the exception for three separate questions to be put on a single amendment. Indeed, for reasons which the reader may prefer to think out for himself, there might be an infinite number of separate questions to be put on a type (c) amendment – and most amendments are of type (c). There might be as many as a dozen divisions on a single motion.

Many Members are unable to be present during the whole course of a debate. They will come in for the crucial division, of course, because they must. They want to record their votes: they want to stand well with the Party. But the reader will have no difficulty in realizing the embarrassment of a Member coming in just after the closure vote on an amendment to the sixth amendment to the Government motion. 'The question I have to put is that the words proposed to be left out stand part of the question.' Which words? What question? Which way is he to vote? Under such circumstances, the whip wears the celestial aura of a guardian angel.

It is a pity that these things are complicated. But procedure designed to meet all emergencies can hardly be expected to be simple. And even amendments have no terrors for a Member who has followed the proceedings and the debate closely.

Types of Motions

One word more on the subject of motions. There are two main kinds of motions: substantive motions; and subsidiary

1. See p. 118.

motions. Substantive motions are capable of expressing an opinion by themselves: they do not depend on any other motion: they do not arise out of any other motion, or out of any other proceeding of the House. Only by means of substantive motions can the actions of certain high personages be discussed: the Sovereign, the Heir to the Throne, the Governors-General of the Dominions, the Lord Chancellor, the Speaker, the Chairman of Ways and Means, Members of either House of Parliament and Judges of the Superior Courts of the United Kingdom. (It should be mentioned that Ambassadors do not, as is sometimes thought, come within this category.) The motions which have so far been used to illustrate this section are all substantive motions. Substantive motions, in fact, are just ordinary motions such as might be moved at any time. When Mr Churchill returned from his last conference with Premier Stalin and President Roosevelt – the meeting which had such a tragic sequel – he put down a substantive motion on the subject of the conference:

That this House approves the declaration of joint policy agreed to by the three great Powers at the Crimea Conference and, in particular, welcomes their determination to maintain unity of action not only in achieving the final defeat of the common enemy but, thereafter, in peace as in war.

Subsidiary motions are somewhat more complicated. They depend upon or relate to other motions, or follow upon some proceeding in the House. Amendments, for instance, are subsidiary motions: so are dilatory motions (when they are strictly dilatory, and not, as often with the adjournment, really substantive motions): and so are the motions by which Bills proceed ('ancillary motions').

The principal differences between the two types of motion are these:

Substantive motions generally require notice, whereas subsidiary motions do not.

No amendment can be offered to a 'dilatory' motion. Such motions must be decided without amendment.

Only certain prescribed formulae may be used in amendments to 'ancillary' motions. In the case of a motion to read a Bill, the amendment may take the form of a 'block', i.e. 'That the Bill be read a second time' (or whatever stage has been reached) 'upon this day six months'. The effect of such an amendment, if carried, is to kill the Bill, since, as will be explained later, in earlier times the parliamentary Session rarely lasted longer than six months. The other alternative is a 'reasoned' amendment, i.e. a motion not to read the Bill, with reasons: 'That this House declines to give a second reading to a Bill which will deprive business men of their right to do what they like with their hard-earned money.'

In Committee, of course, the case is different. There, whole clauses are offered to Bills by way of amendment. The subject of Bills will be more fully discussed later on, in Chapter IV.

Tendencies

It has been explained that the ideal course of deliberation – the decision of the majority on a precisely framed motion – has been superseded, in the House of Commons, in many, if not most cases, by debate on a general topic, precariously attached to a motion such as the adjournment, with a majority assent or dissent indicating support or otherwise for the Government's policy, and that this has been carried to great lengths in the financial procedure of the House – about which more anon. But in at least one important branch of the activity of the House of Commons – namely question-time – even the pretence of a formal motion is not adopted. The House has there only informal methods of expressing clearly its united opinion on a matter. Then only the atmosphere of the House, the asides, the tumult and the shouting can tell the Minister, or the Speaker, how the House feels upon a particular subject. During question-time the House, in a curious way, reverts to the prototype of Parliaments – the *agora*, the market-place, the talking-place, where the rulers and the ruled meet and exchange views. It will be interesting to see how this (modern) tendency develops.

Meanwhile, after this rather dull chapter on fundamentals, we must pass on to consider the daily work of the House, and the rules by which it is conducted.

CHAPTER III

RULES AND ARRANGEMENT OF SITTINGS

HOURS OF SITTING

UNTIL recently, if the enquirer had happened to open the little blue volume entitled 'Standing Orders of the House of Commons' he would have found at the very beginning an order which said categorically that 'unless the House otherwise order, the House shall meet on Monday, Tuesday, Wednesday and Thursday at a quarter to three.' The House, as a matter of fact, *had* otherwise ordered, and indeed had varied the hours of sitting considerably year by year since 1940,[1] in order to avoid sitting at night and presenting a target to the German night bomber. When, at the end of the war, night sittings were once again resumed the hours were stabilized at from 2.30 to 10.30 p.m., in an attempt to avoid the acute strain of excessively late sittings – a vain attempt, as experience has shown. The hours of sitting on Friday remain, as in pre-war days, at from 11.0 a.m. to 4.30 p.m. In either case, as will be seen, the hour of rising is approximate.

The habit of beginning business at a late hour dates from the eighteenth century, and it reflects in a most striking manner the character and interests of the then Members of the House. They were not professional politicians, but ordinary citizens with business to transact or a profession to follow in the outside world. Many of them pleaded in the

1. From 18 September 1940 the House began the practice of meeting at 11 a.m. every day, and rising, first at 4.30, then at 5.30 – or 6.30 in the summer months.

courts or were 'in the City' during the forenoon. This is perhaps no longer usually the case. Being a Member of Parliament is now generally found to be a full-time occupation,
and the salary which, since 1911, has been paid to Members
(with a recent increase) is only one indication of their true
position. But there is still a very good reason for meeting in
the afternoon. It is yet another case of the expanding of some
old habit into new growth for the new need. There is an immense amount of committee work to be done in connexion
with the House; it has always been difficult to hold meetings
of large Committees while the House is itself sitting. Members cannot be in both places at once. And so the mornings
are kept clear for Committees, for interviewing constituents,
and for preparing speeches. Ministers in particular are glad
to have the morning free, both to deal with the work of their
departments and to prepare their answers for question-
time.

The arrangements for ending the sittings are rather more
complicated, and require careful explanation. It used to be
the case, until 1888, that the House sat on until Members
were too tired to talk any more. There was always a danger
of some grossly healthy individuals arriving as fresh as paint
about 10 o'clock, and keeping other Members who had
borne the burden and heat of the day out of bed until the
small hours. Many a man has found his constitution seriously impaired by the strain of assiduous attendance until
late hours. 'Here I am again,' writes Macaulay to his sister
in 1831, 'sitting up in the House of Commons until three
o'clock five days in the week, and getting indigestion at great
dinners the remaining two.' Some famous statesmen seemed
to be specially constituted for this sort of life: Palmerston,
for instance, who was quite as fresh at three o'clock in the
morning as at three o'clock in the afternoon, Sir Robert
Peel, whose capacity for endurance must have been pro-

digious,[1] and Gladstone, whose habit of keeping the House
into the early hours of the morning roused Members to constant fury. The only weapon available to the ordinary
Member against unduly protracted sittings was force of
public opinion: noisiness, coughing, refusal to listen to any
more. The prolonging of a sitting has always been a political
weapon; and no party has been willing to allow that weapon
to be entirely lost. But when the Irish Nationalists began
their concerted campaign of obstruction of business it became essential to introduce some rule to govern the end of a
sitting. On one famous occasion in 1881 the Irish party kept
the House in continuous Session from 4 o'clock on a Monday afternoon until half-past nine on the following Wednesday morning when, as Jennings records, 'the chamber
looked as if it had been the scene of a violent conflict. The
floor was covered with a litter of torn paper. The survivors
were limp and sleepy, and even the higher officials seemed
in a state of abject misery.'

It was as a result of this and similar occurrences that the
present system was instituted. It now provides for a *normal
termination* of business at half-past ten but also leaves a
loop-hole for a very much later sitting when necessary.[2]

First of all there is what is called the 'hour of interruption
of business'. At ten o'clock Mr Speaker rises and calls the
House to order. Any business then proceeding is interrupted,
and a day, named by the Member in charge of it, for its

---

1. Perhaps the last Prime Minister to be thoroughly acquainted with
the work of all the Departments. He habitually worked seventeen hours a
day in his last administration. Rosebery, *Sir Robert Peel*.

2. Present hours of sitting are in strange contrast with those of Parliaments of old. Clarendon (*Rebellion*, I 233) says of the Parliament of 1640:
'the House met always at eight and rose at twelve ... that the committees upon whom lay the greatest burden of the business, might have
the afternoons for their preparation and despatch.' It is evident that he is
speaking of eight a.m. and noon.

resumption, is announced from the Chair. The remaining items of business set down for that day ('Orders of the Day') are then called out by the Clerk, if there is no opposition to them, or if no one wishes to speak upon them, and taken immediately. Otherwise they are postponed to a later day. When all the remaining Orders of the Day have been thus disposed of, half an hour is usually devoted to a debate on the motion 'that this House do now adjourn.' The matters raised in such debates are usually personal or minor grievances, generally arising out of some question which has not been satisfactorily answered at question-time. Then, half an hour after this debate has begun, the Speaker rises and announces 'This House now stands adjourned.'

It has been mentioned that a loophole is left for continuing the sitting until much later than the hours prescribed by the Standing Order. The actual wording of the Order is rather complicated; but if the enquirer has the patience to disentangle its various provisions he will see that the loophole occurs in two places. First of all there is the saving phrase 'unless the House otherwise order.' This is strictly unnecessary, since in any case the House always has power to alter any of its own orders; but it serves to indicate that the framers of the Order contemplated that it would from time to time be altered. Actually the Order (generally referred to as 'the rule') is frequently suspended, in order to allow debates to be carried to their natural conclusion.

Secondly, there are various kinds of business which are not subject to interruption at the hour laid down in the Order. The great financial Bills of the year (the Finance Bill, and the Consolidated Fund Bills) are exempted business,[1] and so are the motions to annul Statutory Instru-

1. The following is the full list of exempted business:

(a) All stages of Bills originating in Committee of Ways and Means and Reports of Committees of the Whole House authorizing expenditure (not of the Committee of Supply).

ments, etc. ('prayers'), which have a nasty habit of cropping up just when everyone is ripe for bed.

Thus it still happens that the House frequently sits very late, in spite of the Standing Order. In March 1907, when debating the Consolidated Fund (No. 1) Bill and the Army and Air Force Annual Bill, the House sat continuously from 2.45 on a Wednesday afternoon until 5.36 on the following Thursday evening. When Mr Lloyd George was fighting his first great budget through the House against bitter opposition (income tax: 9d. in the £1) the Committee stage of the Finance Bill, which embodied the budget proposals, took forty-two days on the floor of the House; and in most cases the sitting was protracted until 3 or 4 in the morning, and, on one occasion, until 8.30 in the morning. On Monday, 11 June 1951, the House sat on till 10.16 p.m. on Tuesday, 12 June, also on the Finance Bill. These are all examples of 'exempted business'. But there are cases too numerous to recount of all-night sittings where 'the rule' has been deliberately suspended. For instance on 7 May 1947 the House continued sitting until 11.47 a.m. the next day, in a gallant attempt to complete the Committee stage of the National Service Bill, and then adjourned without in fact finishing it: and on the following 23 July the sitting on the Lords'

(b) Proceedings in pursuance of an Act of Parliament or Standing Order; particularly motions for an Address to the Crown to annul departmental orders made in pursuance of Acts which expressly provide that an opportunity shall be afforded for such proceedings. (Lord Campion has explained that as such motions are mostly set down by Private Members it is essential that they should be exempted from the normal rules which govern the time of the House. They can thus be taken at the very end of the day. The Government, which arranges the programme of the day, might otherwise be unwilling to give time for their discussion. It should be observed that this particular exemption is not laid down in Standing Orders, but a matter of 'practice'. Where the Government feel that it is being abused, as they have occasionally felt recently, they can move the adjournment of the House on a 'prayer'.)

Amendments to the Transport Bill lasted until 10.50 the following morning.

It has now been ordered that even when the sitting has been thus prolonged beyond the hour of the Standing Order, the precious half-hour of adjournment debate will still come before the House rises. It has also been ordered (and this again is a departure from the original Standing Order) that where there is a division or unopposed business lasting until after the 'hour of interruption' the half-hour will start to run from the conclusion of the division or the unopposed business – i.e. a complete half-hour will in any case be available.

Why, the curious visitor may ask, does the House sit on Friday at eleven and rise at half-past four? There appears to be no reason for this arrangement except the practical one that it allows Members who have homes and constituencies in distant parts of the island to repair to them on Friday evening, without missing any of the day's business. Members who have a train journey of six hours or more each way may reasonably expect a clear two days at their destination when they get there.

THE PROGRAMME OF THE DAY

The House begins its sittings shortly after half-past two in the afternoon, and the visitor who approaches the chamber will notice an air of tense expectancy in the lobbies and the corridors. The crowd of 'strangers' – visitors, journalists, Government officials – are carefully marshalled on either side of a broad gangway, guarded by policemen. Just before Big Ben strikes the half-hour the reason for the excitement becomes clear. The distant shouts which have for some minutes been echoing down the corridors resolve themselves into the word 'Speaker', and in a moment the policemen spring to attention, sweep off their helmets, and cry 'Hats

Off, strangers!' Slowly, and with infinite dignity, the Speaker's procession crosses the lobby,[1] headed by the Chief Badge Messenger and the Serjeant at Arms with the mace. So, with this simple, but strangely moving ceremonial, the head of the sovereign assembly goes to take his place in the chamber. Prayers, read by the Speaker's Chaplain, claim the first attention of the House, Members standing in their places facing the seats; and then the press and visitors are admitted to the galleries, and the day's work begins.

If we disregard Friday, for the moment, we shall find that the programme of the day divides itself roughly into two unequal parts. There is the period from the beginning of the sitting until 3.30 or 3.45, which is occupied mainly by question-time (normally lasting some fifty minutes), and a number of smaller items of business, which do not all occur every day. Then there is the period from about 3.45, when – as a general rule – the Speaker calls upon the Clerk of the House to read out the Orders of the Day, until the end of the sitting. The words 'as a general rule' must be held to indicate here rather more than the usual perplexingly flexible nature of parliamentary procedure. Sometimes – nowadays on certain Fridays – the Orders of the Day are not read out until the end of the sitting, and their place is taken by motions, generally moved by Private Members.

This second period of the sitting day is sometimes interrupted about half-way – i.e. at 7.0 p.m. – whenever a debate on a Private Bill or a Private Member's motion relative to

1. Before the 1939 war the Speaker merely crossed the Members' lobby into the chamber. After the destruction of the chamber and the use of the Lords' chamber as a temporary chamber, the Speaker had to cross the central hall of the building on his way to his chair. This processional appearance was so popular that it has been continued since the opening of the new chamber.

some urgent matter of public importance has been appointed for that day. But generally the business begun at about 3.45 is the main business of the day, and it lasts until the 'hour of interruption', which, as already explained, is usually followed by a half-hour of adjournment debate.

We have thus Part I, from 2.30 until about 3.45; and Part II, from about 3.45 until 10.0. It will be convenient to consider Part I in two separate divisions: (a) before question-time: and (b) after question-time: for question-time is a fixed event which occupies almost the same space of time every day, whereas other items of business are capricious creatures, which have to be hunted for in the pages of *Hansard* or in the index to the Journals. The difference between Friday and the other days of the week is that on Friday there is no question-time at all.

Before question-time (2.30–2.45). One of the difficulties of discussing this most important part of procedure, the daily time-table of the House, is that there is uncertainty as to the proper place of many of the minor items of business. They never all occur together. But in recent practice the following has been the order of business before question-time when the items concerned happened to be taken:

1. Report of the King's answer to addresses.
2. Formal announcements.
3. Motions for new writs.
4. Unopposed private business.
5. Presentation of public petitions.
6. Motions for unopposed returns.

It should be explained that prayers occupy rom 2.30 to about 2.35 p.m., and that the time taken up by all the abovementioned items is rarely more than two or three minutes.

Often nothing at all occurs under any of these six head-ings, and the House proceeds straight from prayers to questions. Unopposed private business is the most regular item in this group, and it must not last beyond 2.45. In any case, as will be explained in Chapter VII, there is not a great deal of private business nowadays. The only item which might take much longer is the moving of new writs – i.e. writs for bye-elections in constituencies where a Member has recently died, or been elevated to the peerage, or other-wise ceased to be an M.P. A recent ruling prevents even this from lasting more than a quarter of an hour here: at 2.50, if the debate on the new writ has not been finished, it is postponed until after question-time: the object being to prevent question-time, perhaps the most valuable hour of the day, from the encroachment of odd pieces of busi-ness.

It may seem odd to those who did not follow the political events of war-time closely that any prolonged debate could develop upon a motion so formal as the moving of a new writ. During the war years, however, the Common-wealth Party frequently challenged the motion on the (very pertinent) ground that the electoral register was out of date. On one occasion the discussion swallowed up half of ques-tion-time, and was responsible for the new ruling referred to above. On another occasion a Member accused the Govern-ment of holding up the moving of a new writ until their own election plans were ready. Whatever the rights and wrongs of the matter, it certainly took up a good deal of time.

The presentation of public petitions, which might seem a fruitful source of debate, is now so hedged round with restrictions that it is insignificant. Not many petitions are presented nowadays: of these, only a few a year receive a word of introduction on the floor of the House. No debate is permitted.[1] In fact public petitions, except when part of a carefully organized parliamentary campaign, appear to be little but a waste of money and energy on the part of the petitioners. The House itself will not, in fact cannot, do anything about them, and their only useful function is to serve as an indication of public opinion. Most of the few petitions which still arrive do not conform to the rules laid down by the House and therefore receive even less attention than they would otherwise attract. It could be wished that the good people who organize them would make sure they follow the rules, before expending time and money on them, by consulting the Clerk to the Committee on Public Petitions beforehand. But for general guidance and at the cost of a slight digression, the following is the substance of the rules:

1. A petition must be addressed to 'the Honourable the Commons of Great Britain and Northern Ireland in Parliament assembled.'
2. It must be respectful and decorous, especially in its references to Parliament and the courts of justice.
3. It must pray for something – i.e. it must be couched in the form of a prayer, not in terms of a demand or an exhortation.
4. It must not ask for a grant of public money, or refer to debates in either House or to motions on the Order Book of the House.

1. It was formerly far otherwise. Thus on 18 July 1838, Gladstone records in his diary that he had complimented the Speaker on his action in putting an end to debates upon the presentation of petitions. 'He replied that there was a more important advantage; that those discussions greatly increased the influence of popular feeling on the deliberations of the House; and that by stopping them he thought a wall was erected against such influence – not as strong as might be wished. Probably some day it might be broken down, but he had done his best to raise it. His maxim was to shut out as far as might be all extrinsic pressure, and then to do freely what was right within doors.'

5. The top sheet of the petition must be written by hand: at least one signature must appear on the same page as the handwritten prayer of the petition: if other sheets are added for additional signatures they must be headed with the prayer of the petition (which may, in this case, be printed).

6. The petition must contain no erasures or interlineations.

All these tests are very strictly applied. The petitioner may well complain that his scope is very much restricted if he may not ask for money for any object, or allude to the constituted authorities in any but the most respectful terms: and indeed it is far more useful to write to an M.P., or better still to several M.P.s, than to sign any petition, however well organized,[1] and a failure to comply with the pure formalities of the rules will lead to a rejection of the petition.

Why does Parliament treat the poor petitioner in this cavalier way? The rigorous code of rules dates from the time when the House was inundated by petitions. Now that the floods of petitions have not merely receded but dried up the code still serves to discourage recourse to a procedure which, though useless, cannot be abolished without infringing what is still technically one of the rights of the subject – free access to the highest courts in the kingdom.

Little more need be said about the rest of the group of items of business which have their place at the beginning of the day. Formal announcements are read out by Mr Speaker. Congratulatory addresses and messages of goodwill from other constitutional bodies form the bulk of them. Perhaps the Bulgarian Chamber of Deputies sends a message of congratulation upon the termination of the recent elections

1. Full lists of rules relating to public petitions can be obtained from the Vote Office or the Journal Office, House of Commons; and they are also set out in the *Manual of Procedure in the Public Business*.

without bloodshed; or Mr Speaker exchanges democratic greetings with Estonia. Motions for 'returns', i.e. figures of statistics, etc., from departments usually cause little trouble in the House, however much to the departments concerned. The other items will become clearer in the course of our consideration of the passage of a Bill through the House.

Question-time (2.35–3.30). All this may take no time at all. By a quarter to three question-time is well under way. It lasts until not later than half-past three. But question-time is a subject of so much importance that it demands a separate Section.[1] It is enough to say that this and the short period after it are, for the average visitor, the most attractive part and for the student of procedure the most interesting part of the parliamentary day.

After question-time (3.30 to about 3.45). During the quarter of an hour after question-time events are apt to become a little confused. Great excitement is generated, and the precise order of things is not easy to distinguish. But the correct order of business, when all the items occur, is as follows:

1. 'Private notice' questions.
2. Statement of business for the coming week, and announcements of other arrangements in connexion with the sittings of the House.
3. Introduction of new Members.
4. Motions for the adjournment of the House under Standing Order No 9.
5. Ballot for notices of motions.
6. Ministerial statements and obituary speeches.
7. Personal explanations.
8. Raising a matter of privilege.

1. See p. 104.

'Private notice' questions and ministerial statements are of a nature akin to question-time. 'Private notice' questions are often put by mutual arrangement, in order to allow Ministers a peg on which to hang a long statement. Frequently they refer to important matters which, it is felt, should not be buried in the brisk interchange of question-time. Thus it was from an answer to a 'private notice' question put to the Foreign Secretary that in January 1944 the world learnt the terrible story of the treatment of British prisoners of war by the Japanese. As the name implies, 'private notice' questions differ from ordinary oral questions in not being printed on the Order Paper; and for this reason they are sometimes used when it is thought desirable to secure a reply immediately, and there is insufficient time to print the question with the rest of the Order Paper. They are also used by the Leader of the Opposition, who does not put questions on the Order Paper.

Not all ministerial statements are made in answer to a 'private notice' question. Often important statements are made without any such pretext; the Minister makes his statement 'by leave of the House'. This is a practice which experienced parliamentarians dislike. It is impossible for the House to debate the matters contained in the statement, and to come to any decision on them, since there is no motion before it on which it could vote. A debate could have no natural termination: it would be a matter of individual expression, rather than the expression of the will of the House. It is therefore necessary to keep a watchful eye even on the extent to which Members may ask questions 'arising out of the statement which we have just heard', or the give and take of questions may develop into a ragged and wrangling debate. Many of these statements may be controversial, and it is not always easy to restrain the barrage of questions afterwards. For instance, it was from such a statement in

June 1944, that the country first learned that the Southern counties were being subjected to bombardment by flying bombs. It was on such an occasion that the House was informed of the sudden surrender of the Belgian army to the Germans, which was such a stunning blow to a public which had been assured that all was going well, when they learned of it on that sunny day in May 1940.

The statement of the business which has been arranged or the ensuing week (generally made on Thursday) takes the form of an answer to a 'private notice' question from the Leader of the Opposition to the Leader of the House. It usually results in a barrage of questions. Almost every Member has some subject dear to his heart which ought to be dealt with in the near future, and here again the Speaker has to use great tact to avoid an irregular debate developing. In fact this whole period is a danger spot. The quick succession of items which arouse general interest raises the temperature very considerably; high words are sometimes exchanged; there is frequently a 'row'. It was at this time of day that in 1931 Mr McGovern was carried out of the chamber by main force, and that, towards the end of the last century, most of the disturbances caused by Mr Bradlaugh occurred.

The Speaker is generally glad of the opportunity to call upon a new Member to take his seat, if only to cool the atmosphere. The Member comes forward humbly, flanked by his two sponsors, bows, signs the test roll, takes the oath, and then shakes hands with Mr Speaker; while the excitement of the previous moment is dissipated in a buzz of general conversation. Sometimes, however, the opposite is the case. Many Members will remember Mr Churchill reading through a long statement upon the welfare of the troops in India to an audience which could hardly conceal its impatience for the end; impatience to see what would happen when the new Member for Motherwell made his second attempt to take his seat. He had attempted to enter and subscribe the roll the day before, without sponsors, since there were no other Members of his own rather exclusive party then in the House, and he was unwilling to accept sponsors from any other party. The House, by an overwhelming majority, had refused to allow him to take his seat in defiance of the rules, and he had to withdraw. A repetition of this rather dramatic struggle was expected on this occasion, but the haughty new Member unexpectedly gave way, and allowed himself to be introduced by two independents. He was defeated at the general election a few months later.

Much more violent was the protracted struggle waged by Mr Bradlaugh in the 1880's against the whole House, a struggle which in one instance ended in the lone hero being carried by force from the chamber and thrown out into New Palace Yard, amid the cheers of his enormous following. Then there was the case of Baron Rothschild in 1858, the first Jew to be introduced as a Jew and to be sworn on the Old Testament.

Motions for the adjournment of the House under Standing Order No. 9 on a definite matter of urgent, public importance are rare, and have become progressively less frequent throughout the century. The reason is not that there is less occasion for such motions, but that the application of the tests of urgency and importance has become more rigid. The opportunity to move the adjournment of the House on a matter of urgent public importance must necessarily be restricted to rare occasions, or the conduct of public business would suffer. There is always a tendency for rare privileges to disappear altogether.[1]

1. Between 1920 and 1930 leave was given for seventeen urgency motions. Between 1930 and 1940 only seven such motions were debated. See as an example of the stringency with which the rule is now applied the attempt of Dr Haden Guest to move the adjournment on the subject of British intervention in Greece, 5 December 1944 (H.C. Deb. 406 360–61).

The procedure is as follows: The mover rises and says, 'Mr Speaker, I beg leave to move the adjournment of the House on a definite matter of urgent public importance, namely', and then states the grounds of his motion. The Speaker, who either has already had a copy of the motion in writing or has called for it when the application was made, must now indicate whether he is prepared to accept it – i.e. whether he considers that it is urgent, definite, and of public importance. If he is ready to accept it he will ask whether it has the leave of the House. If as many as forty Members rise in their places it is assumed that the motion has the leave of the House, and it will come on the floor for debate at 7.0 p.m. If less than forty Members rise, but more than ten, the question of whether leave is granted is put to the vote, and so decided.

The usual style and scope of urgency motions may be gathered from a recent example. On 23 June 1938 Mr Attlee obtained leave to move the adjournment of the House on a definite matter of urgent public importance, namely 'the attacks made yesterday upon British ships and their crews and the refusal of His Majesty's Government either to afford adequate protection or to take measures to prevent their recurrence.' The debate was, as was then usual, appointed for 7.30 p.m. Mr Attlee delivered his speech at 7.30; he was followed by the Prime Minister, and after several other speakers had intervened, the Under-Secretary of State for Foreign Affairs summed up. At eleven o'clock the division was taken, and the motion was defeated, as is usual in these cases, where the Government is attacked, and sends its majority into the division lobbies.[1] A still more recent case was the motion of Mr Clement Davies on 17 July 1947

1. The House had thus resolved not to adjourn; but fifteen minutes later, the business of the day being completed, the adjournment was again moved by the Government and carried.

upon 'the immediate reduction of newsprint to the press.'

Leave to move a motion under Standing Order No. 9 will certainly be refused –

(a) if the matter raised has not just happened, or can be postponed to a later occasion for discussion, or if a motion on the same subject has already been put down [urgent];

(b) if the case is hypothetical, or in general terms, or is not confined to one subject [definite];

(c) if the matter is a purely personal grievance, or one upon which no official information is available[1] [of public importance].

The *sine qua non* about these urgency motions is that they must touch upon some matter for which the Government is in some way responsible. There was some doubt about this point when Mr Baldwin moved the adjournment of the House in 1929–30, on the appointment of a Judge to serve on the Speaker's Electoral Reform Conference. It was suggested that as the nominations to the Conference were made by the various political parties, the Government had no responsibility for the appointment and the mover no *locus standi*. The motion was, however, eventually accepted.

For the visitor who is looking for dramatic episodes there remain two fruitful sources of excitement. It is at this point that Members who feel that they have been misrepresented or slandered come forward to correct the report of their words or to clear their character. It is at this point that Ministers who have resigned from the Government generally explain the grounds of their action to the House. Here too, since there is no formal motion before the House, there is a danger of irregular debate arising. Explanations, therefore,

1. The rules governing question-time apply to a certain extent here (see p. 104).

must be strictly confined to personal matters and not stray into the realm of politics.[1]

Complaints of 'breaches of privilege' have in 1951 become a rather common and often very dramatic feature of parliamentary life. The privileges of the House are regarded as such an important feature of its constitution that any complaint of an infringement of them must, if raised at the earliest possible moment, be given priority over other business. Actually the privileges of individual Members are now so severely restricted (e.g. freedom from arrest, which hardly exists at all now) that breaches of them must be rare. Most cases of 'breach of privilege' are contempts of the House. The House must preserve its own dignity and authority, in order to carry out its functions. Formerly when complaints of 'breach of privilege' were made they were dealt with by the House itself, which passed a resolution, declaring that the matter was or was not a breach of privilege, and ordered the culprit to attend at the bar. Of late years (since 1930) a habit has arisen of expecting the Speaker to rule whether the case is a *prima facie* case of breach of privilege, and if so of referring it to the Committee of Privileges to consider and report upon it. This perhaps saves some time, and allows for a more judicial consideration of the matter. Eventually, however, the House itself alone can decide the matter; it can accept or reject the Committee's findings, so that the time saved here may be lost later on. Also it rather puts the Speaker in the place of a judge, although even if he rules that no *prima facie* case exists, a Member may still put down a motion on it. Many cases raised in 1951 have been rather trivial, but they have engendered much heat.

Before the Commencement of Public Business. There are one or

1. See for instance the report of Mr Stokes's statement of 16 December 1942 and the Speaker's ruling, H.C. Deb. 385, 1934.

two items of business which belong strictly to the second part of the day's sitting, but which frequently seem to mix themselves up in the 'after-questions' period. It is important to observe the correct order in these minor items, since they can hold up the rest of business very considerably, especially if they are taken out of turn.

First of all there may be a presentation of a Bill. This is usually a brief ceremony: it will be more fittingly described in the section upon Public Bills.[1] Then there are the 'business motions' (if any): mostly motions to suspend the rule relating to the length of the sitting, or to vary the order of public business. These motions, though they have to be decided without amendment or debate, are frequently the cause of much excitement. It was not unusual, before the war, for the House to divide upon them every day of the week, just in order to register attendance, and make sure that Members were present at the beginning of the sitting. In days of old the irreverent were wont to aver that some Members came in by taxi for this division, and left immediately afterwards by the same convenient means: and that this was all they ever saw of the House. Such imputations are hardly likely to be incurred by the vigorous parliaments of to-day. Then there are motions for leave to introduce Bills under the 'ten minutes rule' – Standing Order No. 12. It is an interesting and important part of a Private Member's privileges. This again, however, will better be described in Chapter IV, where the method of introducing Bills is explained at length.

Orders of the Day (3.30–10.0). At last we come to the main business of the day. It may be the second reading of a Bill: it may be the debate on a Government motion. One of the Ministers will open the debate, and he will probably be

1. See p. 126.

followed by the Leader of the Opposition. The interest of the House will then slacken, and the attendance will diminish correspondingly. Lesser speakers will arise, and address themselves to the glossy unresponsiveness of empty benches. But though an ungrateful House of Commons prefer the peace of the smoking-room or the clamour of Committees to the sound wisdom of Mr B., the wisdom will not be entirely unappreciated. His friends, and anyone else who is interested, will be able to read it afterwards unabridged in the pages of *Hansard*, either by paying for the weekly edition or for the daily parts, or by borrowing a bound volume from a library.

At 7.0, as already explained, there is an opportunity to interrupt the debate. There may be an opposed Private Bill to be debated, or a motion under Standing Order No. 9. In former days, if it happened to be a Wednesday, the debate on the first Private Member's motion ended at 7.30, and the next motion on the list was called.

Or, on the other hand, the original debate may go on until 10.0 or until later if the House has so ordered it. Attendance will fluctuate considerably. About dinner-time it will become very sparse. During the nineteenth century there was an institution known as 'the Speaker's chop' – i.e. an unofficial interval for dinner, during which the House stood suspended. In 1902 a regular dinner-hour interval from 7.30 until nine o'clock was instituted. This practice was found to have its dangers. It was difficult to get Members back again from a comfortable armchair at home, or a pleasant party elsewhere, and for this and other reasons it was soon abandoned. Nowadays the Speaker has deputies who can take over for him at dinner-time without any order of the House and he is not, as formerly, forced to be in the Chair as long as the House is sitting.[1]

1. During the famous long sitting of 1881, referred to above, the House had to be informed of the 'unavoidable absence' of the Speaker each time he was relieved by his deputy. When, after Dr Playfair had

Friday sittings. This is the course of business upon Mondays, Tuesdays, Wednesdays, and Thursdays. The main difference on Friday is that there are no oral questions, and that the day as a whole is much shorter (about one-half of an ordinary parliamentary day). The sitting does not divide up like an ordinary parliamentary day; and after the ten minutes or so which are absorbed by the miscellaneous items at the very beginning of the day, the business begun lasts solidly until four o'clock.

There is, however, this further difference. Before the war, until about Whitsuntide, every year, Friday and Wednesday were Private Members' days, and were devoted, Friday to discussing Bills presented by Members who were not Members of the Government and Wednesday to discussing motions not sponsored by the Government. Following the Report of the Select Committee on Procedure of 1945–6, this arrangement has been superseded by allocating twenty Fridays of the Session to Private Members' Bills and motions, instead of the former complicated allocation of Wednesdays and Fridays. During the war years, the Govern-

---

deputized for him from 4.50 a.m. until 1.25 p.m. on the second day, Mr Speaker returned to the Chair, Parnell attempted to show this to be irregular. The standing order, he said, required that if the Deputy Speaker took over he had to stay in the Chair for the remainder of the sitting. This argument was soon disposed of, but it is interesting to note that even under those conditions Mr Speaker was not supposed to be relieved without the implicit assent of the House. This was the position until 1909, when the standing order was amended. Even as late as 1853 there was no official Deputy Speaker at all; and a Select Committee in 1853 computed that the House had sat for 13,000 hours, 1,196 of them after midnight, during the Speakership of Shaw-Lefevre. Under such conditions the office of Speaker must have been a very severe test of physical endurance.

Sir H. Lucy records the case of a Member who was mentally deranged, and the final proof of whose insanity came when he went behind the Chair and 'tried to eat the Speaker's Chop'!

ment found it necessary to appropriate all the time of the House, including Fridays and Wednesdays, for their own business, but Private Members have now regained their own time on Fridays.

In a sense all the time of the House is Private Members' time. What is normally called 'Private Members' time' is really the time available to Private Members for initiating, as well as dealing with, business. It is true that the tangible achievements of Private Members in their Private Members' time have not been very great, measured by the vulgar standards of apparent success. A small number of excellent Bills, for which the Government would not take responsibility, have reached the statute book in this way. A number of Bills have been put forward, which, if they had ever reached the statute book, would have seriously embarrassed the administration of justice. And Private Members' motions have never the slightest chance of passing without the support of the Government, unless the Government majority is very low, and the Opposition support them. But, on the other hand, the opportunity for ventilating grievances and letting off steam afforded by Private Members' days is always very valuable.

The arrangement which was recommended by the Select Committee on Procedure, and which has been adopted now is as follows. All Private Members' time is concentrated in the first twenty Fridays of the Session. These are allocated for Private Members' Bills and motions alternately. Ten days are thus occupied for Bills, of which the first six days are devoted to the second reading stage of Bills, the last four to later stages. This is slightly less than the time given to Private Members under the old dispensation, but it is generally recognized that the claims of Government business have become much heavier in recent years, and the reduction in the time devoted to other business must necessarily be curtailed.

If there are only ten days available for the discussion of Private Members' Bills and each Bill needs at least a day for all its stages, and the pockets of some 624 Members are lined with unborn legislation, it is obvious that there must be some process of selection. Accordingly a ballot is held every Session for precedence in presenting Bills. A special ballot sheet is set out in the 'aye' lobby at the beginning of the Session, and Members wishing to take part enter their names in the spaces provided on it. The actual drawing of the ballot is performed in a committee-room upstairs. In the case of motions there is a similar ballot once a fortnight, and the 'draw' takes place in the House on Wednesday after question-time. The last Select Committee on Procedure recommended that these two ballots should be combined in one ballot.

Counting out. The reader will readily suppose that sometimes the sitting will close earlier than had been anticipated. A debate will flag and fail in the most unexpected manner, and in the end there is nothing for it but to put the question on the motion before the House, to move the adjournment, and so to end the proceedings for the day. But the sitting may also be ended in a much more abrupt manner. The House of Commons, like every other properly constituted body, has a quorum, and that quorum is forty. If there are less than forty Members present in the House it is open to any Member to rise and draw the attention of Mr Speaker to the fact. Mr Speaker then rises and says 'Notice having been taken that forty Members are not present, strangers must withdraw.' The division bells are set ringing,[1] and at the end of two minutes Mr Speaker proceeds to count the

1. The bell rings once for a count and four times for a division. As they are ancient and melodious, the process takes some time. They also ring once when the Speaker enters for Prayers, and again after Prayers when he takes the Chair, and when the House rises.

House.[1] By this time sufficient Members will usually have emerged from the odd corners of the Palace to make up far more than the necessary quorum. It is the duty of the Government Whips (except on Private Members' days) to ensure that there is always a 'House' at any rate within call. Sometimes, however, these mysterious functionaries are found wanting: a rival attraction has drawn away all the Members: less than forty are found to be present and the sitting is immediately adjourned.[2] If, as is most unlikely, a count is claimed before 4.0 p.m., the sitting is suspended until 4.0, and the count then taken. It is, however, very rarely that less than forty Members will be present at question-time. Dinner-time (half-past seven to half-past eight according to present arrangements) and lunch-time on Fridays (1.15–2.15) are sacrosanct. A gentleman's agreement used to protect Private Members' Fridays from sudden countings out – otherwise few Fridays would have escaped the combined effect of hostility and indifference to other people's cherished projects. Nowadays it is not infrequent to claim a count on Friday. Finally Mr Speaker will not allow himself to notice the absence of a quorum too soon after the House has been counted already. On a recent occasion a Member tried to force two separate counts within half an hour, as a protest against the inattention of Members to the debate. It seems that he had been counted out himself in

1. It was formerly the practice of Speakers to use their cocked hats as pointers for this purpose. Mr Speaker puts on his hat when reprimanding or admonishing an offender at the bar. (The last occasion of this sort occurred on 30 October 1947, when Mr Heighway and Mr Walkden were reprimanded for offences in connexion with party secrets.) This seems to be the only use he makes of it nowadays.

2. It happened once in 1921, six times in 1922, twice in 1923, five times in 1924, four times in 1925, four times in 1927, once in 1928, and three times in 1929–30. It never occurred in 1926, the year of the general strike. The tempo of political life has naturally a great deal to do with the strength of attendance.

the course of a speech on a previous occasion, and that this was in the nature of a reprisal. His second attempt to secure a count was rejected, and the House took vengeance on him for his persistence by seeing to it that it was counted out again during one of the hon. and gallant Member's speeches a few days later.

Sir Reginald Palgrave, in his lectures on the House of Commons, records the strange case of a Member who counted himself out. Evidently a tedious speaker, he had attracted only a handful of Members to listen to him. Angered by the scanty attendance, says Sir Reginald, 'he joked about the crowded benches, the packed House, that he pretended to see around. The jest was fatal; he had referred to the number present; this done, and the Speaker must determine what the number is. "Order! Order!" from the Chair, silenced the debater. Amazed, he sat down, quite ignorant of the effect of his wit – the Speaker rose in all solemnity, in due custom he began the regular "One, two, three" as his extended arm pointed in stately circuit to each Member. Soon all was over; the two minutes elapsed, but twenty heads were counted, and the House broke up, much in laughter at the luckless orator, who had counted himself out.'[1]

What is the value of the quorum? Originally the intention was that business should not be transacted unless at least forty Members were present; otherwise all kinds of strange legislation might creep into the statute book, and the principle of majority rule would be evaded. Nowadays business is frequently – in fact regularly – transacted in the presence of less than forty Members, and the only advantage of having a quorum and the chance of a 'count' is that it does prevent Members from deserting the precincts and their place of duty too easily. Once again, an old custom has a practical value in a new way – 'new growth for the new need.'

1. The ritual of counting appears to have been slightly different in Palgrave's day.

THE PROGRAMME OF THE SESSION

The programme of the parliamentary year is largely determined by the work which the Government attempts to perform in it. There are, however, certain landmarks which are seen in every Session; recurrent items which bear a deep historical and constitutional significance.

Thus each Session must begin with the *King's Speech*; that is, with a statement by the King of the work with which the Government intends to deal during the coming year. This is the essential part of the elaborate ceremony which attends the State opening of Parliament. Both Houses assemble in the Lords' Chamber; the Peers in their seats; the Commons packed in behind the Speaker at the bar, whither they are summoned by Black Rod; and the King reads his speech to them from the throne. It is invariably followed by a discussion in the House of Commons of the legislation foreshadowed in that statement, in the form of a debate upon an address of thanks to the King for 'his gracious speech' – a debate which usually lasts about six days. Then there is the discussion of the estimates of Government expenditure, which must be sanctioned every year by the House of Commons, in its incarnation as the Committee of Supply. There are also the proposals of the Government for raising the money it has been authorized to spend, which must be exhaustively debated in Committee of Ways and Means (the Budget statement and debate). Finally there is the brief ceremony known as Prorogation, when the King's Speech citing the various events of the past year is read by one of the Lords Commissioners (generally the Lord Chancellor), and Parliament is dismissed till a future day. The Session may be likened to a human body, whose backbone is the financial business of the year, the debate on the Address the skull, and the various Bills and motions the features and external appearance of the flesh which are moulded by the underlying skeleton.

There is no fixed length to the Session. Its length will vary according to the amount of business to be performed, the energy with which Members address themselves to their task, and the amount of opposition offered to the Government proposals. Nor is there any constant date for the meeting of Parliament. It is a matter almost entirely in the hands of the Government. For the last twenty years it has been customary to begin the Session in the autumn, and finish it if possible in July or August, or in some cases in autumn, with a long recess in the summer. Before 1929, on the other hand, the ideal which was aimed at was to begin the Session in February and end it in July, leaving the rest of the year free to Members for pleasure or outside business. For a few years at the beginning of the present century this glorious ideal was actually achieved; but there were numerous occasions both earlier and later when the House found itself unable to complete its business by the end of July, and had to sit on through August and even September. In one very grim Session (1909), the House did not get any recess until November.[1] Even in the nineteenth century voices of protest were raised against the inconvenience of constantly having to sit well into August. Sir Charles Forster, speaking on the subject in 1859 said that he 'would frankly admit that Hon. Members ought not to allow any consideration of ease or comfort to interfere with the discharge of duties which they had voluntarily undertaken, but yet they had a right to expect that those duties should not be rendered unnecessarily severe by their being exposed to the pestilential atmosphere of the overgrown sewer, in the midst of which they had built their House, precisely at the period of the year

1. The Chancellor of the Exchequer in the Liberal Government had proposed a rather revolutionary Budget, which the Opposition were determined to fight to the end.

when its foul abominations had the greatest power.'[1] The suggestion that the House should adjourn for the summer and sit again in the autumn was scouted by Lord Palmerston. 'He had had the misfortune to be present at several autumn Sessions, and he remembered being made exceedingly ill by the state of the House. ... Why, hardly a man could hear himself for coughing, not coughing maliciously to interrupt a Member, but a mere effort of nature, in consequence of physical affections produced by the fog, cold, snow and inclement state of the weather.' Parliament, nevertheless, was destined to sit many a long day in autumn and winter, as the business of legislation grew in magnitude. For the last thirty years the House has sat in every autumn; and in 1928 it was decided to adopt the policy of beginning the Session in autumn, so that autumn sittings have now become an accepted part of the routine of the House.

It is instructive to examine the reasons which led to the change of 1928, since they throw a light on the general arrangement of business during the Session. The matter was examined by a Select Committee in 1914, and again by a Joint Committee in 1924, which latter, interestingly enough, reported against the suggested autumn opening of Parliament. The arguments which were adduced in favour of it may be summed up as follows. It would avoid the crush of business in February and March which resulted from having the debate on the Address and the debate on the financial business which has to be transacted before 31 March (Supplementary Estimates, Votes on Account, Speaker out of the Chair on the Service Estimates – see Chapter VI[2]) happening together in the same two months, together with Private

1. 155 Parl. Deb. 3s. 51ff.
2. i.e. all the business which belongs to the financial year ending 31 March of that year. See below, Chapter VI, for an account of financial legislation.

Members' days, and the opening stages of important Bills. It was suggested that by beginning the Session in autumn it would be possible to have the debate on the Address in the few weeks before Christmas, followed by the second readings of one or two important Bills (which could be sent upstairs to the Standing Committees while the House was busy with the financial business in January, February, and March) and perhaps one or two Estimates. It was proposed to end the Session habitually on 31 July, thus guaranteeing a good summer holiday.

The Clerk of the Parliaments and the Clerk of the House of Commons, who appeared before the Joint Committee of 1924, were hostile to the proposal. They pointed out that the hope of debating any major Bills before Christmas was illusory, since there would not in fact be time to draft and produce them by Christmas. The Clerk of the Parliaments considered that July was not a dignified time to prorogue Parliament, and the Clerk of the House of Commons suggested that it would be impossible to have any Estimates ready for debate before Christmas.

The proposed change was, nevertheless, adopted. In a statement on 7 February 1928 Mr Baldwin announced the intention of his Government to begin the next Session in autumn. The statement is not very clear and it is not easy to discover just what factors outweighed the conclusions of the Joint Committee, but Mr Baldwin was evidently greatly concerned about the accumulation of Bills in their later stages towards the end of the Session under the old system. In any case the new system has since then been a regular feature of parliamentary life. The results are said by some persons, well qualified to judge, to show a great improvement. On the other hand, it has been found in practice that it is really difficult to have major Bills ready for debate before Christmas; that while the House, at the end of the Session, is, as before, extremely busy, at the beginning of the Session it can hardly find enough to keep it properly engaged. Moreover it has been realized that the main pressure of financial business is not before 31 March, but afterwards, when the Budget, the Finance Bill and the allotted Supply days[1] take up a large part of the time of the House. The present system of beginning in the autumn does not help in reducing this congestion. One expedient would be to make the financial year begin in January. The Member of Parliament could then deal with a great deal of financial business on the floor of the House, while the great Bills of the Session were slowly maturing in the draftsman's hands. The suggestion put forward by the Select Committee on Procedure is to spread the Supply days more evenly over the Session, by including more items in their purview.

The matter will perhaps be clearer from a diagram.[2] The pressure of business under the present system may be indicated by the following curve:

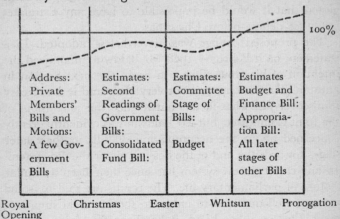

| Address: Private Members' Bills and Motions: A few Government Bills | Estimates: Second Readings of Government Bills: Consolidated Fund Bill: | Estimates: Committee Stage of Bills: Budget | Estimates Budget and Finance Bill: Appropriation Bill: All later stages of other Bills |

Royal Opening   Christmas   Easter   Whitsun   Prorogation

1. When the main Estimates are discussed.
2. The reader might perhaps be well advised to postpone this part of the section until he has read the description of financial procedure in Chapter VI.

(This particular curve is based upon Session 1937–38, when Easter came early: but it represents a fairly average picture of the Session.)

Under the old system the curve would be something like this:

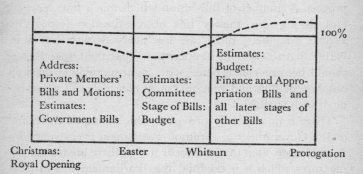

| Address:
Private Members'
Bills and Motions:
Estimates:
Government Bills | Estimates:
Committee
Stage of Bills:
Budget | Estimates:
Budget:
Finance and Appropriation Bills and all later stages of other Bills |

100%

Christmas: Easter   Whitsun   Prorogation
Royal Opening

Since the beginning of the war it has been thought better not to prorogue on 31 July, after all, but merely to adjourn the House for a summer recess, the reason being partly that it was extremely difficult to summon the House together again quickly after a prorogation, whereas during an adjournment the Speaker has power to summon it in case of emergency. This expedient was felt to be necessary during the uneasy years of Nazi expansion. It was also no doubt useful to have a few weeks in November to clear up odd business. In any case the result was that the House was, and still is, solemnly prorogued one day, and solemnly opened again by the King a day or two later, there being now no intervening Christmas holiday.

It may occur to the reader to ask why Parliament is prorogued at all, and why the House should not remain in Session from the time that it is elected until the time that it is dissolved. The natural answer will be that Parliament likes to 'clear its books', just as a business firm clears its books at the end of a financial year. All Bills which have not reached the statute book by the end of the Session are killed automatically by prorogation. All notices of motions disappear from the Order Paper. All Committees disappear and have to be reappointed. It is a drastic but quite salutary process. A number of Bills upon which much time, energy and, it may be, money has been expended (especially Private Members' Bills) are lost every Session, but it is better that this should happen than that the Order Paper should become encumbered with an accumulating mass of obsolescent Bills and motions, most of which will never be dealt with at all.[1]

There is no statutory provision which compels the King or the Government to summon Parliament every year, or, in fact, more often than he needs it. But there are numerous measures which it is essential that Parliament should pass every year, since they are purposely framed to last only one year just in order to force the King – i.e. the Government – to summon Parliament every year. The Act which enables the King to keep an army and an air force in being is one. The Act which compels the payment of income-tax is another. For this reason, and because it is necessary that the House of Commons should sanction the expenditure of public money without which government could not be carried on, every financial year, the House must necessarily meet every year.

We need not attempt, for the moment, to trace the progress of the Session in detail from beginning to end. It has

1. It has also been argued that to take longer than a year to pass a Bill augurs some grave defect in the Bill, i.e. that a Bill which takes longer than a year to pass should not be passed at all. The argument breaks down in the case of the Reform Bill of 1832, but there is certainly something in it. The real trouble is, however, that some Bills are introduced only when the Session is half over. Some Private Bills are kept alive between sessions by passing Standing Orders about them.

already been indicated that much of the business performed in the course of a Session consists of passing votes of money for public expenditure: and the voting of money proceeds according to a rather elaborate system, which will be fully explained in the section on financial legislation. The reader must be reminded of what has already been indicated, and will be repeated *ad nauseam* in the course of this work: namely that there is no necessary connexion between the business performed in Parliament on a given occasion, and the matters debated. So that although the course of the Session takes the shape of the financial framework, which is mostly the same every year, the debates will range over a very diverse series of topics. But the financial framework is still there, and is a very important consideration for the Leader of the House and the Party Whips. Come what may, every year the Estimates must be passed; every year the Budget must be passed; every year the great Financial Bills which are framed in accordance with the Estimates and the Budget must be passed. It is a fundamental principle of the English constitution that redress of grievances must precede 'supply' – and that means in practice that Members must not be prevented from talking, that they must be allowed to state their opinions and to air their grievances, before they grant the Government the money which it needs for its existence, and that this necessarily prolongs the business of voting money. It used to be a formidable weapon in the hands of the Opposition, but Standing Orders have now been made to the effect that twenty-six full days must be spent in Committee of Supply upon the main Estimates of the year, and after that the money must be voted upon without any further argument. This still leaves a certain scope for stating grievances, but as it is no longer possible to state them at such length as formerly, it is not so easy to bring them home to the responsible authorities.

One word ought to be said about the beginning of a new Parliament, as distinct from a new Session. When a new Parliament has been elected there are a number of formalities to be observed. First, a Speaker has to be elected. This is naturally a process requiring tact. The assembly has at this stage no president; there is no one to enforce order or to speak in the name of the whole body of Members. The actual Speaker will usually have been decided beforehand, behind the scenes, and the ceremony in the House is usually just an occasion for congratulatory addresses. The new Speaker is nominated and seconded by back-benchers (i.e. Members not holding any official position) to emphasize the duty of the Speaker to protect minorities, and the complete impartiality of his position. After the candidate has modestly disclaimed the honour to be conferred upon him, he is led by the proposer and seconder to his Chair. He later goes up to the House of Lords to submit himself for royal approval to the Lord's commissioners, and to claim the ancient privileges of his House. After this each Member must take the oath prescribed by law:

I swear by Almighty God that I will be faithful and bear true allegiance to his Majesty King George, his heirs and successors, according to law. So help me God.[1]

After the majority of Members have been sworn, the King opens Parliament, and the work of the Session proceeds in the usual way.

RULES OF DEBATE

Except during the odd moments of excitement, such as blow up occasionally at the end of question-time, the essential characteristic of the conduct and the rules of debate in the

1. Members may, if they have objections to the form of this oath, make an affirmation instead. A Member who is foolish enough to vote in a division without having taken the oath renders himself liable to a penalty of £500 if anyone chooses to prosecute him.

House is a genial urbanity. This, despite Dr Redlich's[1] sug-gestion that it was due to the aristocratic tradition of the House, was never more noticeable than at the present day, in this least patrician of all Parliaments. The past century has seen an enormous improvement in the manners and behaviour of the House of Commons.[2] The reason for it is not easy to trace. Porritt, quoting Sir John Mowbray (the 'father of the House' in Gladstone's day) ascribes it to the strong hand of Speaker Shaw-Lefevre. Perhaps there is no one discernible cause. Like so much else that is good in the institutions of Parliament the behaviour of the House has grown straight, or, like a river, purified itself as it flowed.

Whatever its origin, the spirit of the rules of debate *is*

1. Redlich, op. cit. II, pp. 218-9.

2. Pastor Moritz, a visitor from Germany, has left us this description of the manners of the House of Commons in the late eighteenth century:

'Those who speak', (he says), 'deliver themselves with but little gravity. If a Member rises who is a bad speaker, or if what he says is deemed not sufficiently interesting, so much noise is made, and such bursts of laughter are raised, that he can scarcely distinguish his own words. On the contrary when one, who speaks well and to the purpose, rises, the most perfect silence reigns; and his friends and admirers, one after another, make their approbation known by calling out "Hear him!" '

The following is a newspaper report of a scene in Parliament in 1835, in the days of Melbourne, Russell, Althorp, Palmerston; when it was thought scandalous (says Porritt) that Sir Robert Peel, the son of a rich cotton-spinner, should become Prime Minister:

'The most confused sounds, mysteriously blended, issued from all corners of the House. One Honourable Member near the bar re-peatedly called out "Read" (to the Member endeavouring to address the House) in an exceedingly bass and hoarse sound of voice. At re-peated intervals a sort of drone-like humming, having almost the sound of a distant hand-organ or bagpipes, issued from the back benches; – coughing, sneezing, and ingeniously extended yawning, blended with the other sounds, and produced a *tout ensemble* which we have never heard excelled in the House. A single voice from the minis-terial benches imitated very accurately the yelp of a kennelled hound.'

aristocratic. They are the rules which a body of educated gentlemen would observe when meeting, say, at a rather formal dinner. And if, as is sometimes suggested, the elaborate, rather ceremonious politeness which the rules of the House impose upon its Members tends to obscure the urgency of some of the questions which come before it, if the condition of invalid old-age pensioners and the food situation in Germany seem a little remote amid this courtly atmosphere, who can doubt that it is better that problems should be obscured by politeness rather than be drowned in uproar? Standards of propriety are difficult to fix. It is better that the representatives of the people should be 'Honourable Members' in season and out, than that they should refer to one another by nicknames, endearing or abusive.

Most of the rules, then, are either plain courtesy or common sense. Members must stand up to speak (unless they are prevented by some physical infirmity) and they must speak from their own places – except for those privileged individuals mentioned in Chapter I, who may speak from the despatch-box. The latter rule prevents the fuss and bother which results from having a rostrum into which Members must clamber, and, as already hinted, reduces the amount

Thus the *Morning Post* of 18 July 1835: and James Grant, who quotes it, adds details from his own observation: 'One Honourable Member imitated the crowing of a cock so admirably, that you could not have distinguished it from the performance of a real chanticleer. Not far from the same spot issued sounds marvellously resembling the bleating of a sheep – blended occasionally with an admirable imitation of the braying of an ass by an Honourable Member a few yards distant. There were coughing, yawning, and other vocal performances in infinite variety, and in most discordant chorus. There were yelpings worthy of any canine animal, and excellent imitations of the sounds of sundry instruments not mentioned by the *Morning Post*.' All this was apparently occasioned by the fact that the name of the Member attempting to speak was Hughes Hughes (*Random Recollections of the House of Commons*, by one of No Party, p. 74).

of set oratory delivered in the chamber. A worthy Member of a recent Parliament, who held the opinion that the glory of the despatch-box was due to merit rather than to the mere accident of ministerial prominence, once descended from the back benches to deliver a pronouncement of especial importance from this strategical point. His eminence, however, was short-lived; next day the thunders of the Chair descended upon him, and he did not venture to repeat the performance.

Naturally, gentlemen must speak with heads uncovered. There is one well-known and curious exception. During the progress of a division, if any Member wishes to address the Chair he must sit down and put his hat on. The reason for this convention is stated by Cushing to be that debate at the moment is quite out of order, and that by sitting down and remaining covered a Member makes it quite clear that he is not attempting to deliver a speech. The convention has a practical convenience, in that at that moment everyone else is standing up or moving about and a Member sitting down is therefore more conspicuous. Hats are not usually worn in the House nowadays, and recourse has occasionally been made to the use of ladies hats (by men), Order Papers and the like. The Chair has, however, refused to see the likeness of a hat in a piece of paper held upon a Member's head.

It is out of order to *read* a speech in the House, though there must necessarily be exceptions to the rule.[1] Answers to

---

1. Members still expostulate against read speeches. For instance on 17 May 1944 the following exchange occurred:

Mr McGovern (Glasgow, Shettleston): On a point of Order. Is this really a Debate, or is it a day when Members come here to read prepared lectures? Is not this sort of procedure – by which the Motion is not really debated – undermining Parliament a great deal more than anything else?

Mr Speaker: I noticed that the hon. Gentleman had notes, and he is quite entitled to read notes. I can again take this opportunity of saying that I do not like speeches which are read and which are, after all, against the Rules.

parliamentary questions, which are frequently of a detailed character, involving important pronouncements of policy, may be read; and the Government spokesman opening a debate is generally permitted to use rather full notes, again, as he may be giving utterance to authoritative pronouncements. It is said, perhaps with reason, that the habit of speaking from a written text is growing in present conditions. Certainly it is no new thing. Lord Curzon tells us that Mr Bright spoke from notes concealed in his hat! And Macaulay, whose memory was amazing, learnt his speeches by heart beforehand, and recited them without a hitch, and without having recourse to notes. Mr. Winston Churchill appears to use something of the same technique.

All speeches must be in English. It is on record that a Member once attempted to speak in Irish, but was stopped on the ground that as the Speaker could not understand him he would not know whether he was in order or not!

A Member has a right to be heard without interruption, provided he is not out of order, or irrelevant, or repetitive; in which case Mr Speaker may, under Standing Order No. 20, pull him up. This is done more tactfully than the wording of the Standing Order would suggest, with a wealth of mutual politenesses between the Speaker and the erring Member. A Member has a *right* to be heard without interruption: but by custom (and custom has the force of law in these matters) he will usually yield place for a moment to another Member who wishes to elucidate a point. 'Will the right honourable gentleman permit me . . . ' 'Before the honourable gentleman resumes his seat . . . '[1] The Hon. Member usually resumes his seat for a moment with a show of cheerfulness, while the interrupter states his point. Or, if the hour

1. The point of this remark is that if the previous speaker has really finished his speech, anyone rising to make a point would exhaust his own right of speech for that debate.

is late, and the battle has been fierce, he will perhaps indicate that he is no longer prepared to give way. He may, however, be interrupted 'on a point of order'. There are, of course, Members who at certain stages of the debate seem to become unable to distinguish between points of order and points of substance, and these have to be firmly dealt with.

Then there are other rules which are peculiar to the House of Commons. By an ancient rule, dating from at least the seventeenth century, a Member must not refer to another Member by name, or in the second person: he must refer to him by a descriptive periphrasis in the third person: for instance, 'the honourable Member for Monkseaton' – or, 'the honourable Member who spoke last,' or, 'the honourable Member opposite – has referred to, etc., etc.' 'The noble lord has many striking characteristics and if half of them could be cut out of him the remainder would make a valuable public servant';[1] or 'I am sure the whole House has listened with intense interest to the remarkable speech which has been delivered by the right honourable gentleman.' Privy Councillors are 'right honourable': Commissioned Officers of the three Services 'honourable and gallant': barristers 'honourable and learned'; baronets 'the honourable baronet, the Member for . . . .'; peers,[2] 'the noble lord, the Member for . . . . ' It is not difficult to see justification for these conventions. The delay imposed by the necessity of enunciating the right periphrasis gives Members time to think, and reduces the danger of personal abuse.

One occasion, however, is recorded where a Member was

1. Gladstone, of Lord Randolph Churchill.
2. i.e. Irish Peers, who not being Peers of this Kingdom, are entitled to stand for Parliament, or Peers 'by courtesy' – members of titled families who are not actually themselves Peers – younger sons of Dukes, etc.

referred to in debate, and correctly, by name. The Member was Charles Bradlaugh and the speaker was Lord Randolph Churchill. Bradlaugh, in spite of fierce struggles which reflected little credit on the House, had not yet been allowed to take the oath, and was therefore not strictly entitled to be called 'the Honourable Member for Northampton.' It was interesting to notice that in the more recent (1945) case of Dr MacIntyre, who was not allowed to take the oath without sponsors, this precedent was not followed. In the still more recent case (1950) of the Rev J. G. MacManaway, who was decided to have been incapable of election, Members obviously did not know what to call him in the final debate.

A Member may not speak until his name has been called out by the Speaker – until he has 'caught the Speaker's eye'. Inevitably a number of Members rise to speak as soon as every speech is ended, and the Speaker tries to obtain a representative debate by calling Members from alternative sides of the House, and of various political colours. Usually he has in front of him a list of possible speakers, compiled from various lists submitted to him by the Party Whips.[1] Often old parliamentary hands will write to the Speaker, or have a word with him privately, suggesting that he might fit them into the debate. There are horrible dangers in this practice, especially in new Parliaments. It would be very awkward to allow someone to catch one's eye who was not present at all. But provided the Speaker knows his Members (and he generally does) it works well enough.

Occasionally Members have challenged the decision of the Speaker as to who shall speak next, on the ground that everyone is expecting to hear so-and-so, who has a very

1. This practice has frequently been censured, and perhaps with reason. It is undoubtedly of great practical assistance to the Speaker, but it might easily become a dangerous restriction to debate. Speaker Brand (in 1872) said he had never seen such a list: but they exist, nevertheless.

special contribution to make to the debate. This, however, is quite out of order, and has received effective discouragement.

'Maiden' speeches are given 'high priority' and are usually treated with especial courtesy. On occasion the House has forgotten its manners in this respect. It is well known that Disraeli was shouted down on his first attempt to address the House: and White records the sad case of a Member (Sir Wilfrid Lawson) who attempted to make his maiden speech just as the House was about to adjourn for dinner. He met with a *very* unfavourable reception. Nowadays the manners of the House are better, and such incidents would not occur.

Even where all the usual courtesy has attended a maiden speech, the would-be orator has sometimes failed from sheer nervousness. Parnell and Cobden are cases in point. Some of the greatest parliamentary orators have never managed wholly to conquer their terror of the parliamentary audience. Fox stuttered and stammered at the beginning of every speech and George Tierney (says Macaulay) never rose without his knees knocking together.

Except when the House is sitting in Committee (see below, Chapter V) it is out of order to speak more than once to the same question, even when the debate has been adjourned from a previous day.[1] On the other hand, there are occasions when a rapid succession of different motions has allowed a Member to speak several times in the course of an hour or so – for instance on the first announcement of the loan agreement with America in December 1945 when a Member was able to show that he was in order in speaking

1. 'Which,' says Hatsell, 'is for avoiding replies, and sparing of time, and to avoid heat.' The journals record that Francis Bacon once attempted to speak three times to a question, but was checked the third time (14 May 1604).

several times on the same point (it was very near to his heart) because the adjournment had been moved more than once. It has already been remarked that a Member who has to move or second a motion or an Order of the Day can do so by a formal gesture, and save up his speech for a more propitious moment. Then there are certain exceptions to the rule against speaking twice. A Member may speak a second time *by leave of the House*, so that a Minister could, if necessary, sum up the case for the Government at the end of a debate, and Members may reply to personal attacks upon themselves, or, briefly, to remove some misconception which has arisen in the course of the debate. Then there is a 'point of order' which anyone can rise to put at any time (except when another point of order is being put). And finally during question-time a Member may rise several times to ask questions and supplementary questions; provided that they are questions and not camouflaged speeches.

When a Bill has been amended in Standing Committee (see below, Chapter IV) and is being considered in the House, the Member in charge of the Bill (usually a Minister) may speak more than once, because the report stage of such a Bill is supposed to afford a substitute in some measure for the Committee stage on the floor of the House; and similarly a Member moving amendments to the Bill may speak more than once, for the same reason. Otherwise anyone who has moved or seconded a motion has exhausted his right to speak on that motion, and he cannot move or second an amendment to it. If he has moved or seconded an amendment to the motion before the House he is considered to have exhausted his right to speak on the motion; but he can still speak on the amendment. Thus, by this convention the mover or seconder of an amendment is considered to be speaking on the main motion, not on the amendment – the object doubtless being to reduce the number of amendments moved, or alternatively to prevent second speeches being made under colour of producing an amendment.

Of the list of breaches of order in speaking which the reader will find in the books (May, p. 430 ff., Campion, p. 188 ff.), many are no longer practically considered as such; some are still regarded as serious. It is still quite out of order to 'speak against or reflect upon any determination of the House, unless it is intended to conclude with a motion for rescinding it', to 'utter treasonable or seditious words, or use the King's name irreverently, or to influence the debate', or to 'speak offensive or insulting words against the character or proceedings of either House'. It is quite out of order to reflect upon the conduct of holders of certain high offices, unless a substantive motion on the question is before the House.[1]

It has at various times been ruled to be out of order to 'allude to a debate of the same Session upon any question or Bill not then under discussion', to 'allude to debates in the other House of Parliament', to 'refer to matters pending a judicial decision', to 'make personal allusions to Members of Parliament', and to 'obstruct public business', and although these rules are not always strictly adhered to, they contain a good deal of wisdom. What is essential is that a debate should not be re-opened in the same Session once a decision has been reached, or be dragged on from month to month, unless new and startling information on the subject has just come to light. Similarly the rule against making allusions to a theoretically equal and still powerful body is not without its usefulness. It is not always easy to draw the

1. The officials referred to are: The Sovereign, the Heir to the Throne, the Viceroy of India, a Governor-General of the Dominions, the Lord Chancellor, the Speaker, the Chairman of Ways and Means, Members of either House of Parliament, and Judges of the Superior Courts of the United Kingdom.

line between friendly references and veiled insults: and it is better therefore that there should be no references at all unless a substantive motion before the House makes mention of the matter. The custom of speaking of 'another place' is really an attempt to evade the rule.

Personal allusions to other Members, on the other hand, are part of the small currency of parliamentary debate. Naturally, a line must be drawn somewhere. Members must not impute discreditable motives to other Members; they must not accuse them of deceit or of intentionally misleading the House or the country – unless, of course, there is a motion of censure on their conduct before the House. There has been some variation in the attitudes of different Speakers to different expressions, but two famous Speakers of the last century, Mr Denison and Sir Henry Brand, guided by that great Clerk of the House, Sir Erskine May, ruled the following terms out of order: 'cowardly',[1] 'a poltroon',[2] 'of remarkably fragile honour',[3] 'a bigotted, malevolent young puppy'.[4] On the same authority a Member may not call another Member's words 'the reverse of truth',[5] 'bloodthirsty',[6] 'not credible',[7] 'mendacious',[8] 'a disgraceful statement'[9] or say that he 'has not kept his word'.[10] Allusions to a Member's private life would naturally not be allowed, and the allusions to the physical appearance of other Members which were common in earlier times would nowadays be looked upon as a gross breach of order. It must be remembered that until as late as 1840 any Member who ventured to speak insultingly of another Member was liable to receive a challenge the next morning.

1. 19 March 1867.   2. 2 March 1881.   3. 27 April 1882.
4. 20 February 1884.   5. 28 April 1882.   6. 11 May 1882
7. 15 August 1881.   8. 3 June 1881.   9. 16 February 1883.
10. 3 April 1882. The expression 'the Liverpool Ironmaster' was similarly ruled out.

James Grant, writing in 1835, mentions the case of Hume ('the economist') who was subject to the most virulent and unprovoked abuse from self-advertising Members, because he was 'known to be a man of remarkably peaceable disposition, and not likely either to give or accept a challenge.'[1] The protection formerly afforded by the fear of invoking a duel is now supplied by the rules and the general good sense of the House.

Then there is the question of relevancy, Before 1882, although the Speaker could interrupt a Member who diverged from the subject before the House, his powers were indefinite, and as they carried no particular penalty for the offender, were not much exercised. The real controls upon irrelevant speech were the hostile manifestations of the House, the yawns, the coughs, the cries of 'divide'.[2] This was enough to keep the average Member within the bounds of reason; but it had no effect upon the Irish Nationalists. Their object was to prevent the House doing any business at all until the wrongs of Ireland were righted; and the more noise was made the better they were pleased. Under the circumstances it was necessary to provide some more definite protection for the other Members of the House, and in 1882 a Standing Order was passed empowering Mr Speaker to interrupt any Member 'who persists in irrelevance, or tedious repetition either of his own arguments or of the arguments used by other Members in debate' and to direct him to discontinue his speech. But what is irrelevance? It is mostly a matter for the discretion and good sense of the Speaker or Chairman. Erskine May gives a list of rulings (p. 430) and Lord Campion (p. 190) has formulated some

1. Even Speaker Denison (1857–72) had occasionally to use his influence to prevent a duel between Members who had insulted one another in the House.

2. '2 Maii 1610. A Member speaking, and his Speech seeming impertinent, and there being much Hissing and Spitting, it was conceived for a Rule, *That Mr Speaker may stay impertinent Speeches*' (Scobell).

general principles from it. The following point should be remembered: if the House is discussing a motion to set up machinery to administer a declared policy, it is irrelevant to discuss the policy itself. Thus if the House, having previously accepted the principle of family allowances, were discussing a Bill to regulate the payment of allowances upon a weekly basis, it would not be relevant to enter into a discourse upon the demerits of the principle of family allowances.

In some cases Members have a right to a fairly general discussion: for instance on the motion to adjourn for the recess (in fact on any adjournment motion of a *substantive*, as opposed to a *dilatory* character – see Chapter II) and on the great Financial Bills of the year. There are other cases where a somewhat general discussion has usually been allowed in the past but is by no means a prescriptive right. It was for instance generally accepted that when a Private Bill promoted by a railway company came before the House, Members had a right to raise general points connected with the administration of the railways. But when the London Midland and Scottish Railway Bill, 1944, came up for second reading, and Members tried to raise the question of the relations between the railways and the trade unions, Mr Speaker ruled them out of order on the ground that the Bill only dealt with the closing of one of the company's canals. A 'reasoned' amendment was then proposed 'that this House declines to give a second reading to the Bill' until the railway mended its ways with regard to trades unions. On this amendment the debate proceeded until a Member happened to mention 'the railway companies', and was immediately pulled up by the Speaker. The debate, he said, must be confined to one railway company only, the London Midland and Scottish Railway. After this the debate was carried on uneasily by a transparent substitution of this name whenever 'railway companies' was meant, but Members gradually took more and more licence until it was obvious that the Speaker's ruling had been forgotten. A few days later Mr Speaker gave a very definite ruling to the effect that only railway Bills of a very general character could be made the subject of general debate. Since the nationalization of the railways the problem of debates upon Transport Bills has become even more difficult to define, the scope of British Transport being so enormous. The question of relevance is thus sometimes a little recherché. The right of the matter is not always easy to determine, and Members have been known to enter into somewhat undignified wrangles with the Chair upon the relevance or otherwise of their remarks.[1]

It is not parliamentary to refer in a speech or to quote from documents which are not available to Members – 'not before the House'. Ministers referring to documents are sometimes asked to 'lay them on the Table'. They cannot, however, be asked to lay private correspondence on the Table, and, says Campion, the rule 'may be overridden by considerations affecting the public interest'. Private Members, of course, cannot be asked to lay papers on the Table.

There is, finally, the rule against anticipation. Debate must not cover the ground of a motion which is on the Order

---

1. Here is a case where a problem of relevancy entailed important consequences. In 1858 an attempt was made to assassinate the Emperor Napoleon III of France. The plot was hatched in Britain; but there was no British law by which the assassins could be prosecuted. In reply to a strong despatch from the French Government, Lord Palmerston brought in a Bill to amend the law relating to conspiracy to murder. Was it relevant, on second reading of this Bill, to refer to the French despatch? Speaker Denison ruled that an amendment referring to the despatch was in order, contrary to the advice of his predecessor, Shaw-Lefevre; the amendment was carried, and Lord Palmerston's Government resigned. (Speaker Denison's *Diary*, pp. 11–18).

HC—4

Book, and likely to be discussed. Formerly, even the fact that a motion stood on the Order Paper was enough to prevent debate on the subject it dealt with, and until recently Private Members who wished to prevent the discussion of a particular topic made a practice of putting down motions which they never brought up for debate. Nowadays, however, unless there is a reasonable chance of a motion coming up for debate it cannot prevent Members raising the same subject on another motion.

So much for the Members who are actually speaking. Members who are not actually taking part in the proceedings are naturally expected to behave with decorum. Indeed if all the rules were always strictly followed the deliberations of the House would wear an almost ecclesiastical solemnity. It is technically out of order for a Member to leave his place, or wander about the chamber; to cross the House between the Chair and a speaker; to read books, newspapers or letters; to carry on conversations; to interrupt; or to 'obstruct proceedings'. All these rules are interpreted in the light of common sense. Members are not allowed to stand about inside the chamber proper, it is true; but a throng usually collects at the bar of the House and behind the Speaker's chair, and there is a continual drifting in and out throughout the course of the debate. When crossing between the Chair and a Member speaking, the old parliamentary hands bend low as if to avoid being seen: but even this precaution is often neglected nowadays. Members would not nowadays read books or newspapers while in the chamber, and in this at least the British House can claim to be better-mannered than its American counterpart; but Members have been known to conduct their correspondence there. Gladstone and Disraeli used to write their daily letters to the Queen from the Treasury bench, and some of Macaulay's delightful letters to his sister were evidently written in the chamber.

Macdonagh[1] tells us that in his day a Member would occasionally be seen to slip a newspaper into his Order Paper, so that he appeared to be diligently studying the motion before the House, whereas he was in fact refreshing himself with the gossip column of his favourite daily. Some Members, however, will be seen whiling away the time with the pages of Dod's or Vacher's *Parliamentary Companion*, and thereby combining business with relaxation.

Private conversation, of a subdued kind, is frequently indulged in: indeed it would be difficult to carry on business without an occasional consultation on the front bench. And there are certain interjections which are considered quite parliamentary: e.g. 'Hear! Hear!', 'Divide', 'Oh!', 'Order!', 'Question!'. They can become distinctly unparliamentary. Thus during a recent debate on India, when a Member was summing up with an appeal to the Secretary of State, a certain Member, well versed in obstructive tactics, shouted 'Hear! Hear!' so continuously that the speech became almost inaudible, and the House was adjourned before the speaker could get his point home. This is strictly out of order: and so are cries of 'Shame!', clapping, hissing, and the like. On the whole, the conduct of Members in the House must be just what would be required at any decently-conducted public meeting. There are 'scenes': but they are relatively few. The typical appearance of the House of Commons in action is quiet, if not dull. Such is the typical appearance of the House: but when a Government with a slender majority is in power, and an Opposition is determined to overthrow it, the scene can change more frequently and disconcertingly than this suggests.

By a rather graceful convention, when Mr Speaker rises every Member must sit down. This is, on the whole, an effective means of keeping order. Occasionally it is not sufficient:

1. *Parliament: Its Romance, Its Comedy, Its Pathos*, p. 272.

occasionally a Member defies the Chair, and will not sit down. More drastic action will then become necessary: sometimes Mr Speaker tells the Member he must leave the House for the remainder of the day. Sometimes he is forced to 'name' a Member. 'Naming' a Member was for long a mystery. When Speaker Onslow was asked what he meant when he threatened to name a Member, he replied 'The Lord knows!'. But times have changed. We now know, by repeated experience, what it means. Mr Speaker rises, and calls out 'I must name the Hon. Member for Cork, Mr Parnell, for disregarding the authority of the Chair.' A Government spokesman will then move that Mr Parnell be suspended from the service of the House for a stated period. This being agreed to, with or without a division, unless the Member will withdraw of his own accord, the Serjeant-at-Arms goes up to him and motions him to go with him. If the Member still resists, the badge messengers are summoned to remove him: and as a last resort the police were once brought in.[1]

It is very unusual nowadays for such extreme measures to be resorted to. It is not easy to brave the concentrated anger and disapproval of the House of Commons – did it not make Judge Jeffreys quail? The Irish Members, however, did not care a straw. They courted suspension. On one occasion thirty-seven of them were suspended in the course of a single debate. It then turned out that Parnell had committed a bad tactical error. The motion to introduce the *closure* procedure (see p. 118), which was designed to rob the Irish of their power to obstruct proceedings went through in a single

---

1. The resort to outside aid is, of course, a confession of weakness on the part of a Speaker. Speaker Gully (says Sir John Mowbray) never recovered from the effect of calling in the police to deal with some Irish Members who had defied his authority. He seemed ever afterwards to be unable to assert himself as became his office.

evening, all opposition having removed itself. The Irish could have held it up for days, if they had kept their tempers. On another occasion, Dr Playfair, the then Chairman of Ways and Means, was in such a hurry to suspend the obstructing Members that he read their names out all together from a list, and included the names of two Members who had not been in the House all day!

These are the rules, which every Member must understand. Perhaps this is also a good point at which to mention the essential characteristics of a good House of Commons speaker and debater. First of all, perhaps, there is restraint and modesty. We must realize that a great gulf separates us from the age of Chatham and Burke. The introduction of verbatim reporting, the extension of the franchise, the increase of legislation, have altered the whole character of debate. In place of the leisurely House of Commons of the eighteenth century, dealing with a handful, perhaps not even a handful, of Bills every Session, where a brilliant few spoke, unbridled by fear of press reporting, to the delight of the silent many,[1] we have a House which spends more than half its time discussing the very minutiae of legislation, a House where every word is taken down and telegraphed all over the world in a second, a House where every man fancies himself as a speaker, and no man has time to speak. Passion and unrestricted eloquence are out of place, especially in the young Member. Declamation, thundering invective, glowing rhetoric will for the most part make a man

1. Gibbon, it will be remembered, never spoke in the House, because he despaired of equalling the great speakers. Lord Colchester has the following note in his diary, of 16 May 1797:

'In the House Mr Grey moved a vote of censure on Mr Pitt for his conduct as it appeared upon the report of the Secret Committee. For it, 60; against it, 206.

'Only Mr Grey, Mr Pitt, and Mr Fox spoke. The debate began at half-past six, and lasted till one in the morning.'

merely ridiculous, and though the House can on occasion be lured into enthusiasm, it may be doubted whether any Member of this present Parliament can, *by his speeches*, accomplish it, or can venture even within measurable distance of passionate eloquence; except perhaps Mr Churchill, who unites the advantages of being a great national hero with the longest parliamentary experience in the House of Commons, or, oddly enough, perhaps Mr Aneurin Bevan, who has neither of these advantages.

The House of Commons is a place where a vast quantity of dull and complicated business is performed, under a glare of publicity, by men and women whose occupation it is to perform it. It is filled with people who have something to say and are waiting with consuming impatience for a chance to say it, hoping against hope that the chance will not slip from their grasp. Under these conditions the speaker who is most easily endured is the speaker who is brief, witty, cogent and interesting in argument, and shows marked deference to his audience.

Debate is an even more specialized talent. Macaulay says that the elder Pitt, though a brilliant orator, was not a great debater. 'Scarcely any person has ever become so,' he says, 'without long practice and many failures. It was by slow degrees, as Burke said, that Charles Fox became the most brilliant and powerful debater that ever lived. Charles Fox himself attributed his own success to the resolution which he formed, when very young, of speaking, well or ill, at least once every night. "During five whole Sessions", he used to say, "I spoke every night but one; and I regret only that I did not speak on that night too." Indeed . . . it would be difficult to name any eminent debater who has not made himself a master of his art at the expense of his audience. But,' he continues comfortably, 'as this art is one which even the ablest men have seldom acquired without long practice, so it is one which men of respectable abilities, with assiduous and intrepid practice, seldom fail to acquire.' And Macaulay goes on to point out how odd it was that Pitt did not acquire it.[1]

Unfortunately, assiduous practice in the House itself is not easy, nowadays, owing to the large number of Members who want to speak on every question. It is fortunate therefore, where the anxiety of mutual competition for the Speaker's eye is added to political rancour, that the traditions and rules of the House (and traditions *are* rules in the House of Commons) impose a studied respect and forbearance upon its Members.

It has long been recognized, that, with the growth of the party machine, it has become very difficult, if not impossible, to turn votes by a speech. It never was easy. Macaulay mentions the oration by which Halifax carried the House of Lords against the Bill to exclude James (II) from the throne, as a very rare and signal event in the history of Parliament. Gladstone's thundering denunciations and subtle eloquence prevented his party from breaking to pieces; Disraeli replied so vehemently that on one occasion, as Lord George Hamilton tells us, his false teeth flew out;[2] but it is extremely doubtful whether either of them, *by their speeches*, ever induced Members of the opposite party to desert their whip and join the orator.[3] And now the position is even more

1. *Essay on William Pitt.* The same appears to have been true of Macaulay himself. Macaulay's mind was so stored with information, and his grasp of complicated argument so strong, however, that he was listened to with something like rapture.

2. *Parliamentary Reminiscences and Reflections* 1868–85, p. 43. He deftly caught the teeth in his right hand, and, turning as if to whisper to his neighbour on the bench, replaced them under cover of his handkerchief.

3. It is said that Hartington's speeches against the Irish Home Rule Bill brought over many Liberals to vote against it. Hartington's position, however, was peculiar. He was himself a deserter from the ranks.

difficult, with vigorous party discipline, and an ideological dichotomy in politics. But it is still possible to *persuade* the Government to compromise, to arouse a feeling of discomfort in the opposite benches. And this is much more easily achieved by sound argument than by rhetoric. A good motto for a new Member might be: 'Don't preach; don't argue; explain. And have your facts right.'

QUESTIONS

The first hour of the House, upon every sitting day except Friday, is set aside for questions, usually addressed to Ministers, and to Members with special responsibility, such as the Chairman of the Kitchen Committee. The questions concern matters for which the Government is directly or not too indirectly responsible. They cover the whole field of the nation's life, though the actual scope of them varies immensely from day to day, as the House reacts, barometer-like, to the atmosphere of public life. The discovery of irregularities in a Remand Home, for instance, will bring a swarm of questions to the Home Secretary on to the Order Paper. The agitation of R.A.F. men for demobilization will result in a score of questions to the Air Minister. Generally speaking, the pattern of the questions asked is a compound of the burning topics of the day, sifted (as will be explained later) by the system of ministerial question-days, scandals and accidents fortuitously come to light, such as would fill the middle pages of a responsible evening paper, and private passions of Members.

The machinery of question-time is as follows.

Any Member can 'put down' a question; and he is allowed to ask up to three oral questions a day. The procedure is extremely simple. He must write his question on a piece of paper and hand it in to the Clerks at the Table or to the

'Table Office', or he may send it to the Clerks by post, provided his autograph signature is attached. He must specify the day upon which he desires a reply (though in the case of a 'written' question this does not give him a right to be answered upon that day) and mark the question with a star[1] if he wants an oral answer in the House itself. On days when the House sits, official notice of questions can be given only up to the rising of the House. During a recess questions may be deposited in the 'Table Office' till 4.30 p.m. on the days when the office is open, or they may be sent by post.

The Clerks will examine the question to ensure that it is in order – a matter which we shall consider in a moment. If necessary, they will make minor alterations to the phrasing. It will then go to press, and appear in the 'Vote' (the notice papers) the next day, with all the other notices handed in on that day. It will appear a second time on the Order Paper on the day when it is to be asked, among a long list of others (from 60 to 200 each day) each with a number. Then, when the Speaker calls out the Member's name he will rise and say 'Question number forty-two, sir, to the Secretary of State for Air' (or whoever the question is aimed at), and the Minister will read out the reply which he has prepared with the help of his permanent staff.

When the Minister has answered, the Speaker usually allows the questioner to put 'supplementary' questions 'arising out of the reply'. This often arouses a good deal of

---

1. The star dates from a change made in 1902, when it was arranged that Members could if they wished set down questions for written instead of oral answer. Considerable self-denial, as the reader will readily understand, is entailed in setting down 'unstarred' questions, and not all questions are suitable for this kind of treatment: but there are always some Members who are willing to forego the fame or pleasure of questioning a Minister orally, for the sake of the convenience of their fellow Members.

excitement. Questions, although ostensibly meant to elicit information, are also used for a variety of other purposes; to expose abuses, to ventilate grievances, to extract promises, to embarrass the Government, and some of these purposes can be achieved only by a deft use of 'supplementary' questions. They can be very effective; for though the public departments usually arm their Minister with all the 'supplementary' questions which they can envisage, and suitable replies to them, it is impossible to foresee every contingency: Ministers are frequently cornered, which is unpleasant for the Minister, and, in important matters, for the Government of which he is part. Sometimes more than one 'supplementary' is needed to bring the point home; and here the Member is very much in the hands of the Speaker. If the questions on the paper are very numerous the Speaker will not see the honourable Member when he rises to ask the last, shattering question. Or he may rise and indicate that enough time already has been spent upon the matter. Or again, he may rule that the 'supplementary' ought to be made the subject of another question altogether, or that it is out of order for some other reason.

Supplementary questions are subject to the same rules of order as the original 'notice' questions. They must be framed as questions, and not statements; any Member rising in the heat of the moment to proclaim what he thinks to be true, in spite of what he considers to be the vague evasions of the Treasury bench, will be shouted down with cries of 'Order' or 'Question' from all parts of the House: he is there to ask for information, not to give it. He will, if he is wise, immediately frame his remark as a question, and in this way get it passed. Then, as always, Members must observe courtesy and the proprieties of debate. Long questions are out of order and long replies will not be tolerated by the House: the end of a long answer will be lost in a buzz of conversation, and if a questioner dares to be prolix his words will be smothered in groans. The late Mr Speaker FitzRoy was frequently heard to complain of inordinately long questions and answers.[1] Some latitude, however, is inevitable in asking 'supplementaries'. It is of necessity more difficult to prevent irregularities in questions of which no notice can be given.

If a Member is still not satisfied, or if his questions have shown up some weakness in the ministerial case, he will give notice that he intends to raise the matter in one of the daily adjournment debates, when it can be thoroughly thrashed out. Such debates, being limited to half an hour, are frequently very lively, though the subject is apt to be local and restricted, and the audience few. They may achieve a good deal. Few Members, however, would care to follow the example of the Honourable Member who on one occasion rose and asked Mr Speaker whether, as his question (which was near the end of the list) had not been reached in the time available, and as he knew that the answer was going to be unsatisfactory, he could give notice to raise the matter on the adjournment!

Now what are the rules which are applied to the questions which Members put down on the Order Paper? They are set out in detail in May, pp. 338–48: and Lord Campion has drawn up a list of thirty-eight regulations, which anyone ambitious of asking a question in Parliament should consult (Campion, pp. 149–52). There is also a very useful section on questions in the green *Manual of Procedure in the*

1. Sometimes publicly: e.g. 19 November 1942 and 6 April 1943: 'I think Hon. Members have been asked to try to keep questions down to ten lines, as far as possible'. His successor has often pointed out that the failure to get beyond a certain number of questions in the time allotted is due to supplementary questions and sometimes answers being far too long.

Public Business, which is published by H.M. Stationery Office for the use of Members (7/6). For the purposes of the present study these lists may be further summarized as follows:

1. A question must be short and to the point, concerned with fact and not opinion.[1] It may ask either for information or for action.

2. The subject-matter of a question must be one for which the Government is responsible; and the question can be addressed only to the responsible Minister. It will be obvious that a great number of matters are outside the sphere of parliamentary questions. Apart from the private lives and transactions of citizens, which cannot be the subject of parliamentary questions unless they are the cause of public mischief, a number of matters have been delegated to other constitutional authorities – the Northern Ireland Government for instance – and are therefore not proper subjects for questions at Westminster. Sometimes, too, it is difficult to decide which is the proper Minister to handle a particular question. Questions, if addressed to the wrong Minister, are transferred by agreement to the Minister responsible, and the questioner is informed. This process is often the cause of delay and friction, both for the departments and for the Members, since there are many questions which no one is particularly eager to answer.

3. The language and sentiments of questions must be such as would be admissible at other times in debate. Matters which are out of order in debate will be out of order at question time, – e.g. matters which are upon the order paper for future discussion, invidious references to the Royal Family,[2] to the Courts of Law and

1. 'Questions should not be argumentative, but be so framed as merely to elicit the information asked for.' Anson, *Law and Custom of the Constitution*. Ed. 1922, p. 268.

2. For instance, in May 1858, when the Queen was at Balmoral, Mr Rearden attempted to put down a question in these terms: 'To ask the Prime Minister, as the Queen's health appears to be so weak, that she cannot live in England, whether he has advised her to abdicate in favour

to other privileged persons or bodies, or references to the work of a Committee which has not yet made its report to the House.

4. Questions which have already been asked and fully answered may not be put again in the same Session. If the answer in the first place was temporizing, if new information has come to light on the subject, or if the Member can allege alterations in circumstances he can put down the question again: not otherwise. This is the most frequent ground for the rejection of questions.

5. Questions must not repeat rumours. It is *not* permissible to ask questions such as the following: 'Whether the minister is aware that it is said that all the lions have escaped from the Zoo, and will he take steps to catch them?' A Member cannot ask: 'Whether it is a fact that all the lions have escaped from the Zoo', etc. If a Member hands in a question framed in this way he will probably be asked to change it to: 'Why all the lions were allowed to escape from the Zoo,'[1] etc., so that he takes the responsibility himself for the veracity of the information upon which the question is based.

6. Questions must not repeat newspaper gossip. A Member must not ask: 'Whether the minister has read the statement in the *Daily Star* that the police in Mauritius have recently been armed with rifles, and will he enquire into the reasons for this dangerous innovation?' But he may ask: 'Why the police in Mauritius have recently been armed with rifles?' Questions not founded upon facts *for the accuracy of which the Member himself takes responsibility* are out of order. So are questions asking for expression of opinion or for information available in works of reference. But it is always possible to ask a minister what are his *intentions* with regard to the matters for which he is responsible.

7. Questions must not refer to any debate which has occurred in the current Session.

of the Prince of Wales'. The Speaker refused to allow the question to go on the order paper, though Disraeli, when he heard of it, wanted it to go down so that he could speak in defence of the Queen. It was eventually asked as a 'private notice' question and aroused the deep hostility of the House.

1. Though of course as the Zoo is not under the control of the Government such a question would be disallowed in any case.

8. Public statements may be referred to in questions only when they come under one of the three following headings:

(i) Statements made by a paid servant of a Minister of the Crown in the course of his official duties;

(ii) Statements made by Ministers of foreign countries which have a bearing on British interests;

(iii) Statements made by Ministers – in which case the question (which must be addressed to the Prime Minister) can only be to ask whether the statement represents the policy of the Government.

9. In general, questions must not contain anything which is not absolutely essential to the intelligibility of the subject. No names or statements which could be left out, and particularly no ironical or hypothetical expressions will be allowed to remain in. Even redundancies of expression will be excised by the vigilant Clerks at the Table.

Questions addressed to a particular Minister are assembled together on the Order Paper, so that the Minister will be able to enter the chamber, and after answering his daily quota, slip away back to the ordinary cares of office. But in order that questions to each Minister should sooner or later have a fair chance of an oral reply, the order of these blocks of questions rotates from day to day, so that on one day one Minister answers first, on the next day another, and every Member of the Cabinet has his opportunity in turn. The system by which this is effected is necessarily complicated, and the present writer will not attempt to describe it in detail. There are provisos and exceptions, such as that the Prime Minister's questions must always come about half-way through question-time, together with those of certain other Ministers, according to the day. Since it is often impossible to answer all the questions set down for a particular day in the time available, whatever questions have not been reached by the end of question-time automatically receive a written reply, which is printed in the next edition of *Hansard*.

If, however, the Member concerned still wants an oral reply he can postpone the question instead to a subsequent day.

Members soon learn the art of question-asking. The expert uses his 'notice' question to prise a chink in the masonry of his adversary: then, if the chink is sufficiently wide, he explodes his 'supplementary' with shattering force. For this form of attack, the more seemingly guileless the original question the better. It may even be better to engage a friend to put the 'supplementary' question. It should be remembered that Ministers are not obliged to answer a Member's question in a manner that the Member would consider satisfactory, and there is no appeal to the Speaker that the question has not been fairly answered.[1] The Member must force the Minister to give a better answer by persistence or skill. And often, in the end, even the most discreet Minister loses his head a little, and divulges some of the truth.

There is no test of a Minister's worth so searching as question-time. Nothing brings out his qualities of moral strength and perspicacity so clearly. It is said that Gladstone used to wrap up his answers in such clouds of abstruse reasoning and recondite allusion that his questioners sank back dazed and overwhelmed. There was, on the other hand, a Minister in the war-time Parliament who invariably managed to exasperate and arouse suspicions in his questioners. Even Mr Churchill occasionally allowed his taste for repartee to anger his questioners. But then there are some questioners whom it is hardly in human power to satisfy.

In some ways, questions constitute the most interesting

1. Thus when on 8 July 1943 a Member complained that the Minister had refused to answer his question, it was pointed out to him that he did actually get an answer extending to nine lines of *Hansard* (390 H.C. Deb. 50 2275). Courtesy and the feeling of the House always force the Minister to make *some* reply.

branch of parliamentary work. They have taken the place of public petitions, which, as we have seen, are practically obsolete. And they are a comparatively recent form.[1] Not a single formal question was put to a Minister during the whole of the Session of 1800; while in 1944 158 questions appeared on the Order Paper of 26 September alone.[2] They are a British invention, and they have certain features, such as the prohibition of debate on answer, which are peculiar to this country and the Dominions which have adopted her parliamentary procedure. They are one of the most effective methods of control of the executive ever invented. The terror with which Government Departments regard question-time has to be felt to be believed.

Question-time, of course, is not foolproof. If Members are indolent or hopelessly biased, the questions which they ask will be correspondingly less useful. But, for the most part, the questions on the Order Paper for any sitting reflect the state of mind of the nation on that day, accurately and clearly or less accurately and less clearly, as their representatives are honest and diligent, or less so. In spite of, and in some cases because of, individual failings, question-time is the indispensable Forum of the modern Empire: the flood-lit stage where all the clues are unravelled, and the audience

1. Lord Cowper's question of 9 February 1721 was probably the first question put to a Minister. This was in the House of Lords. It concerned the detention, in Belgium, of an important witness in the South Sea Bubble affair.

2. 'The growth in the number of questions in the House is entirely of recent origin. In the 'sixties and early 'seventies the questions rarely exceeded a dozen, and when they reached twenty the number was quite phenomenal. Writing on 7 April 1879 I find that I used these words: "Probably never were so many questions put in the House as this afternoon. There were twenty-eight on the paper and these were supplemented by twelve or fifteen more".' W. Jeans, *Parliamentary Reminiscences*, p. 135.

see themselves in the actions of the players. Like the eye of the giant in Mr C. S. Lewis's allegory, question-time reveals all the loathly nooks and crannies in the body-politic. It brings out facts, and the knowledge of facts is the root of all good government.

DIVISIONS

We have seen that a majority decision on any question before the House is considered to express the will of the united assembly. Usually the Speaker is able to gather which way the majority opinion lies by a simple process of interrogation and acclamation; occasionally his estimate ('I think the "ayes" have it') is disputed, or rather resisted, and he is forced to call a division.

The starting-point of a division is the order 'Clear the lobbies.' When this order is given the exit doors of the division lobbies which run down each side of the chamber are locked. The electric bells which run all round the Palace are set clanging by the doorkeeper of the House: policemen call 'Division' down all the corridors: there is immense excitement. From all the distant crannies of the Palace, and even outside it,[1] streams the host of Members, surges into the chamber, and through the chamber into the division lobbies beyond. After two minutes the lobbies are thronged with Members, and at this point the Speaker puts the question again. The second putting of the question is important,[2] since it often happens that by this time the resolution of the

1. Some Members have, or had, division bells, connected with the House circuit, installed in their houses in Westminster.

2. The second putting of the question, with the extra two (formerly three) minutes which it gives Members to reach the chamber, is a fairly modern innovation. Speaker Brand was of the opinion that it had acted to the detriment of parliamentary debate by lessening the tension immediately preceding the taking of the vote. See G. O. Trevelyan, *George III and Charles James Fox*, vol. I, p. 52 note.

opposition fails them, and the Speaker's conjecture (I think the 'ayes' have it) is allowed to pass uncontested. The division is then called off. Sometimes the opposition is so small that it is unable to provide the two tellers necessary for the division, and then too, the division is called off. Usually, however, the result is the same as before, and the Speaker accordingly announces the names of the tellers, which have been supplied to him by the Whips. Two tellers are appointed from the 'ayes' and two from the 'noes', one of each for each lobby, to ensure that no suspicion can attach to the counting. Then the exit doors of the lobbies are opened, and the Members file out, past the desks, where they give their names to the clerks, and past the tellers, who count them aloud.[1]

There is, however, one other alternative. If the opposition is obviously frivolous, the Speaker can ask both sides to stand up in turn, so that the result of the voting can be announced without further delay. This procedure has not however been much used in the past, because it imposes an unfair burden on the Speaker.

After six minutes from the first putting of the question the entrances to the lobbies are locked, so that although there

---

1. Burnet's anecdote on the subject of tellers is widely quoted, but is perhaps too good not to be repeated once again. Here it is, in the historian's own words:

'The former Parliament had passed a very strict Act for the due execution of the Habeas Corpus, which was, indeed, all they did. It was carried by an odd artifice in the House of Lords. Lord Grey and Lord Norris were named to be the tellers. Lord Norris, being a man subject to vapours, was not at all times attentive to what he was doing; so, a very fat Lord coming in, Lord Grey counted him for ten, as a jest at first, but seeing Lord Norris had not observed it, he went on with his misreckoning of ten. So it was reported to the House and declared that they who were for the Bill were the majority, though it, indeed, went on the other side. And by this means the Bill passed.'

are generally still Members filing out from the lobbies, no more may enter. When the tellers have made sure that there is no one left uncounted in the lobby, they enter the chamber and inform the Clerks at the Table of the respective numbers. The results are then ceremonially announced to the House by the senior teller for the majority and by the Speaker, the four tellers lining up in front of the Chair and bowing.[1] A burst of cheering generally follows the announcement, as Members relieve their pent-up feelings, and sometimes there are ironical cries to the Government to resign.

It will be seen from the above description that a division cannot possibly occupy less than six minutes by this method. As a matter of fact the time usually taken is about ten minutes. This is quite an appreciable amount, and aggregates several days in the course of a Session. In the course of a recent (rather long) sitting on the Finance Bill, 1951, there were 25 divisions, and the total time which they occupied was thus in the neighbourhood of four hours, which is a considerable part of a precious parliamentary day. For this reason much criticism has been levelled at the system by which the divisions are taken. Exception has also been taken to the physical strain which it imposes on the more elderly Members, not to speak of the indignity of their being herded together in a struggling queue in the division lobby.[2]

1. The tellers line up in the following order facing the Speaker, from right to left: senior teller for the majority, junior teller for the majority, senior teller for the minority, junior teller for the minority. They have previously given in their numbers to the Clerks at the Table, who write them out and hand the slip of paper to the senior teller for the majority. The Speaker then announces the result and the figures.

2. On 20–21 March 1907 there were no fewer than forty-two divisions in the course of a single sitting. On a basis of ten minutes each this would appear to amount to an aggregate of over seven hours of the sitting which were devoted to tramping through the lobbies.

Why then, is some change not made? Setting aside for the moment the question of whether, in an assembly where so much depends upon concession and compromise, it *ought* to be made easy to divide the House, and whether the process of voting on a contested issue ought to be made any swifter than it is, let us remember that the system in use in the British House of Commons does enable the names of the voters on every question to be recorded, an advantage which, in a chamber where there are no fixed seats, would be extremely difficult to encompass by any other method. It is a fact that of all the systems now in use in the democratic world, this is the most efficient and reliable. There is no other system known which so completely provides against fraud and mistakes, even taking into account the immensely long and tedious process of calling the roll, which is in use in the United States House of Representatives. There are, it is true, numerous systems of electrical recording which give an almost instantaneous result, but they are all liable to fraud and practical joking, and they are mostly inapplicable to a chamber where there are no fixed places for Members.

It is possible that some improvement might be made in the present system. One or two mechanical or semi-mechanical systems have been suggested which are applicable to the arrangements of the present chamber, but it is not clear that the saving by any of these means would be very great, or even that there would certainly be any saving at all.

The Standing Order at present limits the duration of a division to a minimum of six minutes: i.e. it gives Members just six minutes to get into the division lobby from the sounding of the first division bell: so that without cutting down the amount of notice of a division it would be impossible to speed up a division by more than about four minutes.

It might be possible, by applying the power of the Speaker to make Members claiming a division stand up in their places (Standing Order No. 34), to avoid quite a percentage of the divisions which now take place: but this, as mentioned above, is open to objection.

The whole question was reviewed by the Select Committee on Procedure of 1946, which reported against any alterations in the present system.

Meanwhile the recording of divisions is not without its humorous side. Members occasionally stray into the wrong lobby, and then have to rush back into the chamber and through into the other lobby to put the matter right. Sir Henry Lucy records an instance of a conscientious Member who heard the division bells sounding as he was wallowing in one of the large copper baths which Mr Herbert Gladstone installed in the Palace towards the end of last century. Nothing daunted, he leapt out, swathed a large towel round his person, and reached the lobby in time to record his vote amidst great acclamation. And in 1889 a Member who was caught by the division bell while he was changing into evening dress in a private room rushed downstairs half-dressed, snatched an overcoat from the cloakroom, and so muffled up entered the division lobby in decency.

CLOSURE AND GUILLOTINE

About 1880, when Parnell and the Irish party were pursuing their systematic campaign of obstructing the business of Parliament, there was much said and much written of the possibility of revising the methods of procedure, which then allowed a question, once proposed, to be debated as long as there was any Member left with anything to say upon it. One suggestion, made with much misgiving and reluctance, was that a system which was then in use in France, and which was known as *clôture*, should be applied, with some modification, in Britain. But *clôture* was a foreign system and had an un-English flavour of arbitrary domination. It might long have remained on the other side of the Channel had not Speaker Brand been forced to apply it himself without any sanction at all in the course of the famous long sitting mentioned above, in February 1881. On the following day *clôture* was made one of the rules of the House, and in 1882 it was embodied in a Standing Order. As time went on the French name was dropped, and an English translation took its place – closure. It was, as we have seen, originally an emergency measure; it is now part of the established procedure of the House. It was intended only as a measure against obstruction by the wild Irishmen. It was said that under no circumstances would it be used against a legitimate opposition. It is now used against the opposition as a matter of course.

The present method of closure is as follows: After a debate has gone on for some time any Member may rise and claim to move[1] 'That the question be now put.' Sometimes Mr Speaker has to think very hard over this. He has to avoid any appearance of smothering justifiable opposition. He has to interpret the feeling of the House correctly. He may refuse to accept the motion. If he does accept it, the question must be put on it immediately, without amendment or debate. If it is negatived, the debate goes on as before: if it is carried, and provided that at least 100 Members vote for it, the question on the motion which was before the House when the Member intervened must be put immediately, and the debate thus ended.

The broad outlines of the closure procedure are thus extremely simple. There are, however, one or two ramifications which ought to be mentioned. There is for instance a

1. What happens in practice is that he rises and attempts to move 'That the question be now put'. The Speaker either allows or disallows the motion.

slight difference in the procedure when closure is applied to the debate on an amendment to the main question. The closure is claimed in the ordinary way, and the question is immediately put on the amendment; but the closure may then be applied to the main question much more expeditiously. A Member will rise to claim, not *to move* that the question be now put, but simply that the question be now put; there is no intervening motion: the onus of applying the closure rests entirely on the Speaker, and not on the House.

Thus (to speak algebraically) if a question X is before the House, and an amendment Y has been moved to it, and is under discussion, a Member may rise and claim *to move* that the question (Y) be now put. This, let us say, is accepted: the question that the question be now put is put and carried; the question on the amendment Y is then immediately put and carried. A Member may then rise and claim that the main question X be now put – i.e. he asks the Speaker to put the question without further debate; and the Speaker will, if he considers that the subject-matter of X has been sufficiently debated [on the amendment Y] put the question X immediately. This procedure applies to all the other questions, if there is a series of dependent motions before the House (e.g. an amendment to an amendment).

Then there are the complications which ensue when the closure is moved at the time of interruption of business. For an explanation of these, however, the reader should consult Lord Campion's work, where the business of closure is very fully discussed.

Closure motions are now a very frequent feature of debate. It is quite usual for the House to divide on a closure motion, and then again on the original question immediately afterwards. But where the Government sponsors a closure motion to a debate on one of its own motions, it will send its majority through the division lobby in each case;

and so the names of Members voting on each side in the first division may be repeated exactly in the second. The result of the second division will accord with the result of the first division. It has therefore been suggested (very plausibly) that the putting of the original question after closure has been carried in these cases should be abandoned, since the result can be exactly predicted, and that if closure is carried in such a case, the decision of the House on the original question should be announced accordingly without further delay.

A development of the closure procedure, known as *closure by compartments* or 'guillotine', is used when it is anticipated that a Bill will arouse fierce and lengthy opposition, and is designed to prevent the Government's programme being thrown out of gear by immoderately lengthy proceedings on one particular measure.

What happens is that when a Bill – such as the Licensing Bill of 1908, or the Trade Disputes and Trades Unions Bill of 1927 or the Iron and Steel Bill of 1948–9 – looks like being very 'sticky', a resolution is passed prescribing a maximum of time to be spent on each stage, and providing that at the end of that period the Speaker (or the Chairman of Ways and Means) shall put the question or questions necessary to bring that stage to a conclusion without further debate. The resolution, which will be in several sections, according to the number of stages involved, will run something like this:

That proceedings on the Committee Stage, Report Stage and Third Reading of the Safeguarding of Industries Bill shall be proceeded with and brought to a conclusion in the manner hereinafter mentioned.

(i) *The Committee Stage*

Five allotted days shall be given to the Committee Stage of the Bill, and the proceedings on each allotted day shall be those shown in the second column of the following Table, and those proceedings shall, if not previously brought to a conclusion, be brought to a conclusion at the time shown in the third column of that Table, etc., etc.

The resolution will go on to specify what is meant by an allotted day.

'Guillotine' motions are thus frequently very long and complicated. The debate on them is often fierce and protracted, sometimes occupying several days, for they are measures specifically designed to cut the claws of the opposition, and render it all but powerless. Before the introduction of the closure, though a minority could not entirely prevent what they considered injudicious legislation, they could hold it up for so long that the Government would be forced to make concessions in order to save its programme. This bulwark has fallen, and the power of the Government over the House is as absolute as the loyalty of its supporters is constant. But even the closure, drastic though it may be, is not such an extreme exercise of arbitrary power as the 'guillotine'. A closure motion has to be passed when a question is actually before the House, and there are scores of disappointed Government supporters, pregnant with undelivered speeches, who will find it a sore frustration of their ambitions. A 'guillotine' motion is passed in advance, in cold blood, and makes the debate itself practically ineffective, because the great weapon of delay is removed before the debate is even begun. Undoubtedly, however, the guillotine is a very present help to harassed Governments in time of urgency and trouble. The argument of expediency may be immoral but it is certainly very compelling.

The guillotine motion has now, on the recommendation of the Select Committee on Procedure of 1946, been extended to the operations of Standing Committees.[1]

1 . But the motion to impose the guillotine on a Bill in a Standing Committee must be passed in the House itself in each case.

THE ORDER PAPER

A word must be said about the bundle of green-blue paper, sometimes known as the *Order Paper*, or, more accurately, as the *Vote*, which is issued on the morning of every sitting day except Monday, as well as on Saturday. It includes the record of the business transacted during the previous sitting, a programme of business for the day, including a list of questions to be asked of Ministers, and a list of motions and amendments which have been 'tabled' by Members.

The top sheets consist of the minutes of the previous day. It is headed 'Votes and Proceedings of the House of Commons', and is sometimes known as the *Votes*, or sometimes, confusingly, as the *Vote*. The inexperienced reader should not expect to derive very much illumination from this document. A good deal of it is taken up by entries which record the deposit of obscure documents 'on the table of the House' – mostly reports or orders of one kind or another made under various Acts of Parliament. The entries which record the business actually transacted are couched in rather archaic English, and give the very barest outline of fact. If the business transacted was a proceeding on a Bill, the entry will merely record the name of the Bill and the stage passed; if a great debate took place on the motion for the adjournment, the entry will merely record the motion for the adjournment and the name of the Whip who moved it. In short, it is a record of what was done by the House of Commons, as opposed to what was spoken by individual Members, which is recounted in the pages of *Hansard*. All these entries are rigidly formalized according to precedent. They reappear in a slightly expanded and still more archaic form in the annual *Journal* of the House of Commons.

The next sheet in the bundle is headed 'Private Business', and is a list of Private Bills (see Chapter VII) set down for consideration, with the various stages for which they are set down.

Next comes the Order Paper proper. First of all, there is a list of questions to Ministers numbered and grouped so that all the questions to each Minister appear together. This presents no difficulty to the most casual reader. But after it comes a heading 'Notices of Motions and Orders of the Day.' This is the official programme of the day. It consists largely of a list of names of Bills with the stages which they are due to pass when next considered – second reading, third reading, etc. These are known as *orders of the day* because they have been ordered by the House to be considered upon this day. The Government are strictly obliged to take the items in the order in which they appear.

So far, so good. Unfortunately, the business actually done on an item may be, and often is, merely a postponement of the item to a future day (usually 'to-morrow') when it again appears on an order of the day. Moreover, the House is not obliged to deal with all the 'orders' which appear on the paper, and very seldom does. Among the items usually appear the words 'Supply – Committee' followed by 'Ways and Means – Committee'. These items have become a sort of punctuation mark. The experienced reader knows immediately that the items above 'Supply' will be taken that day, and those below will not be taken that day. This curious arrangement makes it possible to keep the entire business of the House, present and future, as far as it is known, on the Order Paper, so that even if it is not to be dealt with that day, or even that week or that month, it is not lost sight of. On the other hand, it is a little confusing to the inexperienced reader. This function of the item 'Supply' is often not realized by quite old Members of the House.

Occasionally, 'Supply' appears as the first order of the day. But, unless it is preceded by a little 'a', it is not intended to form part of the business of the day. In such cases, it is usually the intention of the House to debate some business upon a motion for the adjournment, no hint of which appears on the Order Paper, apart from the fact that 'Supply' appears first among the 'orders', without the 'a' which denotes that it is 'effective'.

If, on the other hand, the word 'Supply' does appear first among the 'orders' preceded by an 'a', it indicates that the House will that day resolve itself into Committee of Supply to consider certain estimates of public expenditure which will be found enumerated briefly, in a bracket after the word 'Committee', and in greater detail at the end of the orders of the day, under a number which corresponds to the position of 'Supply' among the 'orders' – No 1, if, as would normally be the case, 'Supply' comes first.

At the end of the 'orders' comes a heading 'Notices of motions relating to orders of the day.' These usually consist of amendments to the Bills which appear among the orders. Such amendments (known as 'tags') appear under a number which relates to the position of the 'order' on which they depend. Here, as just mentioned, appears the notice of what estimates are to be taken in Committee of Supply when 'Supply' is an 'effective' order of the day.

The remaining sheets of the Vote consist of notices of questions, motions and amendments given the previous day, amendment papers for Bills in Committee of the whole House, minutes of Standing Committees, and amendment papers for Bills in Standing Committees.

It will be seen that the Order Paper is by no means a simple, or indeed a very easily intelligible, affair. Undoubtedly, it is not as abstruse as might appear on first sight. It embodies a great deal of the procedure of the House. It is, to a certain extent, the pivot on which the whole colossal machine revolves. It is the actual repository of the intangible things which the House handles. The long list of Bills and motions has a crucial importance. But it is difficult to resist the argument that there is room for experiment in the methods and arrangement of the Order Paper. A Member ought to be able to see at a glance what is the business of the day. It ought not to require any specialized study merely to understand what the various papers refer to. Above all, the actual business of the House ought to appear on the Order Paper and be distinguished from the merely nominal business. This is a matter which will doubtless attract the attention of energetic Members and officials of the House in years to come.

CHAPTER IV

HOW A BILL BECOMES AN ACT

WE have now considered the way in which Parliament transacts its business; and we must turn our attention to the sort of business which it transacts.

If we were asked in an unguarded moment what Parliament *does* we should most of us say 'it makes laws'. This was the conception of Parliament which appealed to the genial and clear-headed lawyer, Maitland. 'The chief function of Parliament,' says Maitland, 'is to make statutes.' Now it is true that Parliament has a great many other functions. It has to vote money for the service of the Government (though this too, is finally ratified by a statute). It has a most important duty of criticizing the executive Government, of bringing to light abuses, of ventilating grievances, of preventing the Government from exercising arbitrary power: and in the minds of scholars and procedural writers this duty has almost eclipsed the legislative function of Parliament. Bagehot places legislation last among the functions he allocates to Parliament,[1] and more recent critics have even suggested that Parliament should become an avowedly criticizing body, and leave law-making to professional lawyers in the service of the Government. The common man would consider this a strange suggestion. He conceives of Parliament as a place where laws are made. And the fact is that the very essence of Parliament is its power to make statute law. Indeed much of the force of the criticizing power of the House is derived from this fact: that it is a body which can, by means of passing laws, do anything it likes.

1. *The English Constitution*, No. 5.

There is nothing that it cannot do – even the celebrated dictum that Parliament can do anything but make man woman and woman man does not indicate a limitation of jurisdiction, but merely a limitation of human possibility. When war broke out in 1939, Parliament, by a series of laws, handed over the entire lives and property of citizens to the executive Government to deal with according to its needs. Parliament, by means of a law, seized upon all men of military age, and took them away from their homes and their professions. Parliament, by means of a law, stopped all trading with Germany at all. And it is *only* in the legislative process that Parliament has this omnipotence. 'The Sovereignty of Parliament,' says Anson, 'is displayed in legislation.' All Parliament's functions, in short, depend upon the power of passing laws. Otherwise its criticisms would have little more effect than those of say, the Trades Union Congress or the British Association.[1]

We must further observe that the process of making statute law, i.e. of passing Acts, is the business of Parliament as a whole – Crown, Lords and Commons. The House of Commons by itself can do nothing except order its personal servants about, and pass pious resolutions that so-and-so 'is expedient', or 'ought to be': whereas the King, the House of Lords, and the House of Commons acting together are all-powerful: they can make law.[2] On the other hand, the House

1. The matter may be put like this. It is useless to give orders unless the orders are going to be carried out; unless machinery exists for carrying them out. In this country the citizens will not obey any orders unless imposed upon them by laws. They can be forced to observe laws by the established machinery of the law-courts. But only Parliament can make law, or give power to other bodies to make law. This refers, of course, only to 'law' in the sense indicated – legislation, or statute law. To a certain extent the day-to-day decisions of the courts, in interpreting statutes and common law, also make law – case-law, as it is called.

2. But see below, pp. 156 ff.

of Commons can initiate measures which eventually pass through the other House and receive the King's consent as laws. And as a matter of fact most of the great contentious and important laws do originate in the House of Commons. The power of the House of Commons therefore over legislation would seem to be very great, and of the Member of that House correspondingly so. The House can fail to pass a measure; the Member can speak against it, can vote against it.

Of course the real position is not quite so simple as that. Members of the various parties in the House of Commons are expected to speak and vote according to the plan of campaign of the party leaders. It follows that if the Government in power – i.e. the leaders of the party which has the majority – bring in a Bill, the other Members of the party will be expected to vote for it. Even if one or two Members show an independent spirit and refuse to follow the party whip, the mass of the obedient Members will be so overwhelming[1] that the adverse votes will not affect the issue. So that, generally speaking, laws introduced by the Government are passed, and usually passed in the form in which the Government introduced them.

There are exceptions. Occasions have arisen when the House of Commons as a whole has been so ill-disposed to a measure that the Government, rather than risk dissension among the members of its own party, has withdrawn the measure, or considerably modified it. This happened, for instance, in the case of Sir John Gorst's Education Bill of 1896, which was withdrawn in the face of the bitter criticism of the Opposition. Sometimes (though rarely) a speech will have so powerful an effect upon the House that for the same reason the Government will be forced to withdraw or

---

1. It is not a mere matter of blind obedience. The policy of the party leaders is the policy of the party members, and the leaders usually know best how to carry it out.

modify a measure under consideration. The Copyright Bill of 1842, for instance, was defeated by a few votes, and it was generally recognized that Macaulay's brilliant speech against it turned the tide.

In the same way few measures not introduced by the Government – measures introduced by the Opposition, or by Private Members – ever become law. The scales are heavily weighted against them. In the first place the Government takes up most of the time of the House for its own business, so that a Private Member has to be more than fortunate to get enough time to take a Bill through all its stages before the end of the Session. In the second place it is difficult for a Private Member to organize a majority favourable towards his Bill – or, as is more usually the case, to prevent a majority of unfavourable Members voting against it. But here again there are exceptions. Every Session, in normal times, a handful of very minor laws introduced by Private Members takes its place on the statute book.[1] Occasionally a Private Member who is unusually popular, or remarkable in other ways, will, by sheer pertinacity, steer an important Bill through the dangerous seas of sectarian animosity, past the Scylla of hostility, the Charybdis of indifference. Sir Alan Herbert's Marriage Bill of 1937 is the most famous of recent examples: and there have been others – for example Lubbock's Bank Holiday Bill of 1871. Sometimes the Government is persuaded to take up a Private Member's Bill by the sheer force of opinion in the House. Thus in 1898, after several attempts to promote a Private Bill to regulate the conferring of benefices in the Church had been frustrated by circumstance, Balfour was induced to

1. In 1901, 153 Private Members' Bills were introduced: 4 became law; in 1902, 168 were introduced: 15 became law; in 1903, 166 were introduced: 12 became law; in 1904, 146 were introduced: 11 became law; in 1950–51, 32 were introduced: 9 have now become law.

HC–5

embody the matter in a Government Bill. But there are other reasons why Private Members rarely succeed in making law, which will become clear shortly.

Laws are frequently 'tidied up' during their passage through the House of Commons. The fierce heat of debate shows up the little flaws which the draftsman has overlooked. A Member may be clever enough to notice a point which the expert lawyer who drafted the Bill has failed to notice, and persuasive enough to induce the Government to attend to it. Sometimes a Member will be able to show so well that in some respect the Bill offends or neglects fundamental principle that the Bill is amended. And for the most part this is the extent of the influence of the ordinary Member of Parliament upon legislation, except for the indirect pressure which he, as a member of the party, brings to bear upon the party leaders. 'It is not merely a question of Cabinet initiative and direction', says Sir Sidney Low, 'but of Cabinet authority over legislation, almost unrestrained.'[1] This is no place to discuss the merits of the question, but the reader ought not rashly to assume that the present position is wholly bad. The Cabinet which shapes laws has the responsibility of administering them, and of seeing that they work. There is no such salutary obligation upon the ordinary Private Member. But that is an argument against extensive Private Member's legislation; it does not apply to the exceptional moment, when the Private Member comes into his own, and he is able to introduce or amend an important measure, because in such cases the Government of the day must take the responsibility.

Every law begins as a *Bill*, which is supposed to be read three times in each House of Parliament, and to receive the King's consent. It is then known as an Act. Why there should be three readings of a Bill is difficult to say: except

1. But see Jennings' *Cabinet Government*. The matter was canvassed before the Select Committee on Procedure, 1931.

that it may be assumed that if the House has given its assent to a measure three times there can be no question of unpremeditated acquiescence to it. The practice of reading a Bill three times dates from medieval times, when the number three was regarded with especial reverence; and by the end of the sixteenth century it appears to have become invariable. It is, after all, a sensible practice: but it is merely a practice, and not a legal necessity. An Act would be no less binding if it had only received, say, one reading in each House. On one occasion in 1945 (it happened on VE day) two Bills, by an oversight, were given a fourth reading in the House of Commons. But of course the 'reading' of Bills is not a matter of reading the text of the Bill, which nowadays is printed and available to all Members, but merely an occasion for debate upon the subject or details of the Bill. And there are various complications which must be described in detail. Different kinds of Bills require different treatment. There are contentious Bills and non-contentious Bills: there are Money Bills and other Bills: there are Commons Bills and Lords Bills.

Kinds of Bills

There is one differentiation which is fundamental. Bills are either (1) Public Bills, or
  (2) Private Bills.

Private Bills (or, to be more accurate, Local, Private and Personal Bills) are not usually promoted by Members of Parliament, but by outside persons or bodies; they confer special powers upon companies, corporations, and private persons. They are not generally of public concern. A city corporation, for instance, which wished to extend the city boundaries, would promote a Private Bill. If the Mumbles Pier and Railway Company want to enlarge the area of their pier, and the South Wales Transport Company, which owns the land adjacent to the pier, refuses to sell, then the Mumbles Pier and Railway Company must promote a Private Bill in Parliament to compel the Transport Company to be what they consider reasonable. The procedure governing Private Bills is wholly different from that governing Public Bills, and it will be further considered in a later chapter.

Private Bills must not be confused with Private Members' Bills. The latter are simply Public Bills promoted by Members of Parliament who are not Members of the Government. Private Members' Bills also will be considered more fully a little later.

Public Bills are, as their name implies, Bills which affect the public; Bills in fact, which are not Local or Private Bills. And for the moment we shall confine our attention to ordinary Public Bills promoted by the Government.

Preliminaries

One of the reasons why so few important laws introduced by Private Members are passed is that there is an enormous amount of trouble involved in preparing a Bill. In the first place to draft a document so that it will convey exactly the meaning it is intended to convey and not, by any stretch of interpretation, another meaning, even in the tension of law-court proceedings, so that it will say what has to be said adequately and clearly, and not say anything it is not meant to say, is a highly skilled task, only to be undertaken by a lawyer who has specialized in that sort of work for years. In the second place every new Act that is passed, in a highly developed society such as ours, is bound to interfere with someone's happiness and peace of mind, and to trench upon established interests somewhere. Sectional interests have to be consulted, if possible met, or failing that soothed. No one, not even the Government, can afford to ignore or trample upon these various groupings of opinion. There is always the next general election to be remembered. So that there must be endless negotiations, deputations and interviews, before even the form of the Bill is settled.

In the case of the ordinary Government Bill, what usually happens is that at a Cabinet meeting a proposal to introduce a Bill to do so and so is put forward by the Minister in whose province so and so lies. It may be part of the party programme, in which case it will be readily accepted. It may on the other hand be a piece of legislation which the permanent officials of the department have been pressing on their various political heads for years: in which case the Minister may have something of a struggle to get his colleagues to agree to give it the necessary time on the floor of the House. If the Cabinet decides to accept the proposal, a memorandum is sent to the Office of the Parliamentary Counsel, containing a general description of the scope of the Bill. The Parliamentary Counsel are the skilled lawyers who draw up Government Bills. Though nominally Treasury officials they are all, when appointed, barristers of considerable standing, carefully hand-picked by the chief Parliamentary Counsel, and expected to make of their profession a religion. (Their duties are extremely exacting; in fact they have been described by a former Parliamentary Counsel as 'slavery'.[1]) The Parliamentary Counsel draw up the Bill on the lines suggested by the memorandum. The draft Bill is laid before the Cabinet for their approval, printed and discussed with the representatives of the principal interests affected. One group may be dissatisfied, and the Bill will have to be redrafted: when redrafted, it may arouse opposition in another quarter, and need further redrafting. It is nothing for a draft Bill to be reprinted as many as fifteen times; and all this, it should be understood, before it even reaches Parliament at all. The process may occupy anything

1. In evidence before the Select Committee on Procedure of 1931.

up to three months, at the end of which the Bill may have to receive Cabinet approval once again.

Something of the difficulties which face the private adventurer into legislation will now be plain. Unless he is unusually gifted he will not be able to draft his own Bill. The Parliamentary Counsel will not draft it for him: they are Government officials only. He must engage a private firm of solicitors to draft it; a firm which specializes in parliamentary work. He will not be able to make use of the machinery which is available to the Government for consulting representative interests, and securing their co-operation. He may not be able to afford to circulate printed drafts or even typed drafts of the Bill.

It will be observed that these difficulties, though restricting, are by no means insuperable. The Private Member will always find the officers of the House ready to advise him; and though they may not be able to draft his Bill for him, they will probably be able to tell him what steps to take.

Introduction and First Reading

Eventually the Minister will be satisfied that the Bill can safely be offered to Parliament, and he will ask the Whips for time in the House. If the Session is young, there will be no difficulty: but if it is nearing May or June the Bill may have to wait for a new Session. It may never be introduced at all.

There are two ways of introducing a Bill. It can be introduced on a motion, or it can be introduced on written notice. The former procedure has almost fallen into disuse now, as far as Government Bills are concerned, and we may disregard it for the moment, and concentrate on the latter and normal method, which is prescribed in Standing Order No 35.

On the appointed day an entry will appear on the Order Paper, just after the list of oral questions and under the heading 'At the commencement of public business'. The entry will give the long title and the short title of the Bill and the name of the Minister introducing it. When the proper moment is reached the Speaker will call upon him: he will rise and bow, and the Clerk will read out the short title of the Bill from a 'dummy Bill' which has been laid upon the Table. At the request of the Speaker the Minister names a day for second reading, and the Speaker repeats it to the House. These proceedings, which take only a moment, constitute the first reading of the Bill. There can be no debate, for there is no motion before the House. Under this procedure debate is saved up for the later stages: but we shall see that under the alternative procedure debate can and does take place at this point, and the House sometimes divides.

Second Reading

Before second reading, the Bill is published, and Members have their first opportunity to study its terms. Negotiations will still be proceeding behind the scenes with various interested parties; proposed amendments will be drafted on behalf of Private Members and the Minister in charge. When the day eventually arrives which the Government have chosen for second reading, the Minister in charge of the Bill will rise and move 'That the Bill be now read a second time.' He will proceed to make his main speech in favour of the Bill, explaining what the proposed measure will do, and how it has come about that it is necessary to do it. The Leader of the Opposition, or some other prominent Opposition spokesman, will follow him, and after the Opposition leader Private Members will speak, and the debate will continue until it is summed up by the Minister (who, it will be remembered, has a claim to be allowed to speak twice on such an occasion) or by some other Member of the Government, usually a Parliamentary Under-Secretary.

Second reading is generally accepted to be the most important stage of the Bill. It is then that the main principles of the Bill are stated, attacked, and vindicated. It is the Bill as a whole which is discussed. Consequently it is out of order to move amendments to the Bill itself. Amendments are proposed on second reading not to the Bill, but to the motion 'That the Bill be now read a second time.' This motion is one of the group of what Lord Campion has described as 'ancillary motions', and only certain kinds of amendments may be made to it, the object of which is to throw out the Bill entirely. It is out of order to propose a direct negative: the usual amendment proposed is either (a) 'that the Bill be read a second time upon this day six months' (when the Session would, under the old conditions, have finished) or (b) 'that this House declines to give a second reading to a Bill which' etc. (stating the reasons for objection). If either of these amendments is carried or if the original motion 'that the Bill be now read a second time' is not carried, the Bill is dead, and cannot be revived until the next Session.

At the beginning of the debate the Speaker will usually indicate whether he proposes to call for debate any of the amendments that stand on the Order Paper. Because of the restrictions on the scope of amendment just described it is unusual for there to be many amendments against a Bill on second reading: usually if there is any, it is the official Opposition amendment, and the debate takes place on that. Otherwise debate takes place on the simple motion 'That the Bill be now read a second time,' and, as is well known, the debate is often very long and heated. It might take as much as three days: but this would be the case of an unusually contentious Bill. Eight days were spent upon the second reading of Gladstone's Home Rule Bill: but this was a Bill of constitutional importance. Usually the Government 'find it impossible to give more than' one day, or two days at the most, to a Bill: and if the Opposition persist in being difficult after that, the closure is applied and the debate forcibly terminated.

For reasons already indicated, a Government Bill is hardly ever defeated on second reading. But in some cases (e.g. the Coal Mines Bill of 1936) so much opposition has been aroused on second reading that the Government have thought it wiser to withdraw the Bill than to force it through. A second reading defeat is, of course, equivalent to a vote of censure on the Government. When the University Education (Ireland) Bill was thrown out on second reading by three votes in 1873, Gladstone immediately resigned; though as Disraeli refused to take office he had to remain Prime Minister, until, in 1874, he suddenly dissolved Parliament, and was badly beaten at the polls: and Peel took the opportunity of a defeat on the second reading of the 1846 Coercion Bill to make the resignation which had become inevitable, owing to the change of his opinions on the Corn Law question.

Committee Stage

Upon being read a second time, ordinary Public Bills[1] go automatically to one of the Standing Committees, unless some Member rises immediately after second reading and moves that the Bill be committed to a Committee of the Whole House or to a Select Committee.[2]

1. The exceptions are Bills for imposing taxes, Consolidated Fund Bills, and Provisional Order Bills.
2. Sometimes 'instructions' are moved after second reading – e.g. 'That it be an instruction to the Committee on the Bill that they have power to extend the Bill to Ireland' (Ministry of Health Bill, 1919). Instructions can be used either to extend or to circumscribe the powers of the Committee.

The constitution and procedure of these various Committees will be described in the following chapter, and little need be said about them here. The purpose of the Committee stage is the discussion of the Bill in detail. Every clause must be put separately to the Committee and accepted, amended or rejected, with or without debate. Discussion in Committee is generally of a very restrained, persuasive character. The Minister is generally terse and quiet, and the speeches of the critics have something of the same dry, businesslike flavour:

Mr. B: I beg to move, in page 2, line 28, after 'statement', to insert 'and map'.

The amendment is a very simple one. Sub-section (4) as at present drafted reads:

An application . . . shall be accompanied by such statement . . . indicating the manner in which it is intended that the land . . . should be laid out.

The Committee will readily agree that a verbal statement, however precise and carefully worded, cannot give an adequate and clear impression of what is proposed. I hope that it is not necessary for me to argue this at any length and that the Minister will find his way to accept the Amendment.

Committee proceedings are not therefore usually very interesting for the visitor.[1]

In spite of this, the Government has to keep a watchful eye upon the proceedings in Committee, and enforce a discipline similar to that employed in the House itself. Occasionally the storms of second reading will invade the Committee. Owing to the smaller attendance and, in the Standing Committees, the small number of Members, combined with the detailed nature of the work, party alignments are

1. It was considered a particular mark of Gladstone's intense assiduity that he habitually came and listened to the speeches in Committee, when other Ministers were only too glad to absent themselves.

weakened and the Government is sometimes defeated on a point. This happened in the case of the Education Bill in 1944, the National Insurance (Industrial Injuries) Bill in 1945 and the Sea Fish Industry Bill in 1951. Sometimes there is a knot of irreconcilable opposition in a Committee. This can be very unpleasant for the Government Whips, since Committee procedure offers supreme opportunities for obstruction. A Member may speak any number of times to the same question, and there are Members who have brought talking at great length without being exactly repetitive or demonstrably irrelevant to a fine art. To such tactics the Government will reply by imposing a 'Guillotine' motion, or by moving the closure on every amendment. This is a salutary if not a drastic remedy: and yet it cannot prevent obstruction. On every clause the Chairman has to put the question 'That Clause – stand part [of the Bill],' and of course, a question has to be put on every amendment, if not several questions. If the Opposition feel so disposed they will force a division on every clause and every amendment. In Standing Committee on the Cinematograph Films Bill, 1927, a minority of six Members divided the Committee no fewer than three hundred times, and prolonged the Committee stage from April to July: twenty-five sitting days. In 1948 the Opposition prolonged the debate on the Gas Bill for months in Committee, and even forced several all-night sittings on the Bill – the only case where a Standing Committee has sat all night. Were this to happen to every Government Bill the Government's programme would soon be unworkable.[1]

1. The chances of holding up proceedings in Standing Committee are much reduced since the extension of the 'guillotine' procedure to Standing Committees. The opposition can still be very tiresome to the Government – as in the case of the Gas Bill, which was not 'guillotined' – but they cannot seriously hold up a big Bill.

If a Bill has passed second reading stage, its fundamental principles are supposed to have been accepted, and whatever alteration is made to the Bill in Committee should be alteration of detail. It is therefore out of order to propose an amendment in Committee which would negative the effect of the Bill, to leave out the only effective clause, or to insert words which would make the Bill have the opposite effect to that which was intended. Similarly amendments which are not strictly relevant to the subject-matter of the Bill, and amendments which are out of line with the general intention of the Bill are out of order. Then amendments must not be inconsistent with whatever has already been agreed in Committee on the Bill, and they must not be trifling, vague, or jesting. It is not in order to propose to leave out a clause, since Members have always the opportunity to vote against the motion that the clause stand part of the Bill.

Nevertheless the cumulative effect of amendments is sometimes such that the nature and purport of the Bill is wholly changed. It is usual for such Bills to be withdrawn – generally after the Committee has reported.[1]

Throughout the long, slow process of Committee Stage, the Parliamentary Counsel who drafted the Bill must attend in the official's box, ready to advise the Minister as to the effect of proposed amendments, or to lend his expert assistance in drawing up a proper formula to embody some accepted alteration. It is his task even before the Bill has been committed to envisage all possible criticisms, to anticipate all the amendments which are likely to be offered, and to consider the effect which they might have on the whole structure of the Bill. Representatives from the appropriate

1. Thus, when the Speaker ruled that if the amendments which the Government intended to make to the Franchise Bill of 1913 (including the introduction of Woman Suffrage) were made the Bill would have to be withdrawn, the Government withdrew the Bill in Committee.

Government department must also be present, to assist the Minister with first-hand information whenever necessary.

Here again, the position of the Private Member of Parliament is much less favourable than that of the Minister. He has the assistance of neither the Parliamentary Counsel nor the representatives of the Civil Service. He must draft his own amendments, unless he can afford to engage the services of a firm of parliamentary agents, or unless he is supported by some powerful outside body which is interested in the Bill, and will engage a parliamentary agent to assist the Members who represent its views in the House.[1] Parliamentary agents are generally solicitors who have specialized in the very intricate matter of law and practice of Parliament; they are primarily concerned with Private Bills, but they find an occasional excursion into Public Business a very lucrative addition to their more normal activities.

Report Stage

When the Committee has concluded its deliberations the chairman must put the question 'That I do report the Bill as amended to the House' or 'That I do report the Bill without amendment to the House.' It might be very awkward if this motion were negatived: the Standing Committee would not be carrying out its task. Actually it is always agreed to. The Committee then hand the Bill back to the House, with or without amendment. In the case of a Committee of the whole House it will be realized that as the Committee and the House are one and the same body, and meet in the same room, the process is purely symbolic. The Chairman calls out 'Order! Order!' and leaves the Chair; the Mace is replaced on the Table; the Speaker, or, more usually, the

1. Thus, during the passage of the Requisitioned Land and War Works Bill through the Commons in 1945, the Commons and Open Spaces Preservation Society engaged the services of a very old-established firm of parliamentary agents to watch its interests.

Deputy Speaker assumes the Speaker's Chair; and the Chairman, or one of the Chairmen's Panel, or a Whip, bows to the Chair, and says, 'I beg to report that the Committee have gone through the Bill and directed me to report the same without amendment', or 'I beg to report that the Committee have gone through the Bill and made amendments thereunto.' The Speaker then enquires 'Bill to be considered – ?' and the Whip supplies him with the desired date. In the case of other Committees, the report is handed in at the Table by a clerk – the name written on a printed form.

The vital difference between the consideration of a Bill by Committee of the whole House and the consideration of a Bill by a Standing Committee or other select body is that in the latter case there must always be a debate in the House upon Report (report of the Bill to the House), whereas the report of a Committee of the whole House is not debated unless the Bill has been amended.[1] The theory behind this practice is that the whole House must have some opportunity of considering the Bill in detail, and making amendments to particular clauses, which they would not otherwise have in the case of a Bill reported from a Committee of fifty members. For the discussion upon report is like the discussion in Committee, essentially a discussion of details, as opposed to a discussion of basic principles.

There are certain peculiarities of this consideration or (as it is usually called) 'report' stage. The debate on the Bill begins as soon as the order for consideration is read out by the Clerk (unless, that is, the Member in charge of the

---

1. For this reason, in Committee on the Education Bill of 1898, Balfour, with admirable tenacity, resisted all amendments. His object was to save the time which a report-stage would have cost on a contentious Bill, and so enable the Bill to come into operation in time to furnish grants for schools in the current year.

Bill calls out 'Tomorrow' or some other future day). No question is put on the Bill as a whole: nor is the question put on every clause. New clauses[1] are debated before anything else: then the Bill as amended is discussed. Amendments moved on report must be relevant to the Bill, and they must not have the effect of negativing the whole of it, or of leaving out its principal provisions. Members may move that the Bill be recommitted; and this is regularly done when a Bill has been reported from a Select Committee or a Joint Committee because the whole body of Members must have an opportunity of criticism in detail.

Normally 'report' stage does not arouse great excitement. As, however, it is the last occasion on which amendments of substance may be made to the Bill, the Government sometimes avails itself of the opportunity to make amendments which were promised at an earlier stage and have taken time to draft, or for some other reason were only put on the paper and not moved: and amendments which it is felt are of such importance that they ought not to be made in Committee. But frequently the House passes straight from report stage to third reading on the same day. The scope of debate on third reading being somewhat different from that on report, this practice has some odd effects. Upon the report of one Bill from Committee, in 1943, a Member rose to make some general observations upon the Bill. The Deputy Speaker, who was then in the Chair, pulled him up. The Member[2] was making a third reading speech, he said. The Member sat down, and no other Member attempting to rise, the order for third reading was immediately read out: and he rose again and made exactly the same speech

1. Notice must be given of the intention to move a new clause on 'report' stage.

2. The late Mr Maxton.

with a sly allusion which aroused an appreciative chuckle from his hearers.

Third Reading

The rules governing third reading are substantially those which apply to second reading: and except for the fact that the scope of debate on third reading is more restricted than on second reading, and may not go beyond the matter in the Bill, it may follow much the same course as the debate on second reading, with all its excitement. The third reading of the great Education Bill of 1906, for instance, was a great occasion. Feeling ran high on both sides, and there were very rousing speeches by Augustine Birrell, who was in charge of the Bill, and Balfour, who led the opposition to it. This, however, was rather a special case. Opposition to the Bill was stiffened by religious enthusiasm; and although the Government had a sufficient majority to carry it easily through the Commons, the majority of the Peers were known to be hostile. This third reading debate was rather like a farewell party to a famous though not universally popular figure, about to undertake a dangerous voyage; and as a matter of fact the Bill was eventually killed by the amendments made to it by the Lords, which the Government could not accept. The recent nationalization Bills (especially the Iron and Steel Bill) had very tense third reading debates.

Most third readings are very different from this. The Education Bill of 1944 affords a striking contrast. This Bill passed its third reading without a division, though a highly contentious measure: the fight was already fought, the victory won, the spoils divided. On this occasion the speeches were mostly expressive of the congratulations of Members to the Minister who had steered the Bill safely through the storms of second reading and Committee.

The procedure on third reading is exactly similar to the procedure on second reading. No amendments can be offered to the text of the Bill, except for purely verbal or drafting amendments; and opposition is expressed by 'blocking' or 'reasoned' amendments. The question is put in just the same way as on second reading; but, if the question is carried, the Bill, instead of being committed, is immediately sent up to the Lords. The Clerk carries the 'House Copy', tied up with red tape (the colour of their Lordships' House) and it passes out of the ken of the faithful Commons.

Lords' Amendments

The Bill passes through much the same stages in the Lords as in the Commons. If their Lordships have no amendments to offer to it the Bill becomes an Act without further ado, and the Commons see no more of it, until they are summoned to attend the Royal Commission which affixes the King's consent to it. If their Lordships dislike the Bill they may amend it considerably or even throw it out altogether, like the first Reform Bill of 1831, the Finance Bill of 1909, and the Parliament Bill of 1947. They are unlikely to throw out Bills sent up by a Conservative Ministry, for there has always been, for the last century, a Conservative majority among the Peers upon whom the Ministry can rely for support. The increased severity of the Parliament Act (see below) has made vigorous interference by the Lords rather futile. They may, however, make amendments, and these amendments have to be submitted to the Commons for approval, just as, in the case of a Bill originating in the Lords, amendments made thereto by the Commons must go back to the Lords for approval. Frequently the Government will take the opportunity offered by the passage of the Bill through the Lords to enable amendments to be made to their own Bills — generally slight matters of drafting, or amendments consequential upon amendments already made. Sometimes the Lords, in a moment of restlessness or recklessness, may make amendments of substance, and this will lead to trouble.[1]

A Bill amended in the other House comes back to the Commons automatically, and the Member in charge of it sets the Lords' amendments down for consideration upon a convenient day. It now stands upon the Order Paper as an Order of the Day, and is read out at the appointed time by the Clerk. The Speaker then puts the question 'That the Lords' amendments be now considered.' This is generally agreed to without any fuss; though it is in order to move a 'blocking amendment' (e.g. 'upon this day six months') to it. The Clerk next proceeds to read out the amendments one by one, and as each amendment is read out the Minister or Member in charge rises and moves 'That the House doth agree with the Lords in the said amendment.' In most cases agreement is obtained readily enough, and the difficulty is to read the amendments sufficiently quickly: but here and there the House will stumble over some amendment, or the Minister will find it prudent to explain it. Sometimes the Member in charge of the Bill, resenting an amendment made by the Lords, will move 'That this House doth *dis-agree* with the Lords in the said amendment': sometimes the motion to agree is negatived. In such cases a Committee is appointed to 'draw up reasons' for not agreeing to the amendment: a more or less formal proceeding. Then an exchange of messages takes place between the two Houses, and if the Commons insist on their disagreement to the

1. Quite considerable amendments were made by the Lords to the Education Bill of 1944, but in this case they were accepted without much heat. More recently the Lords made some amendments to a Bill which introduced financial charges: such matters being the privilege of the Commons, the Bill was 'laid aside'.

Lords' amendments to their Bill and the Lords will not let them go, or the Lords insist on their disagreement to the Commons' amendments to their Bill, the Bill is lost.

Sometimes amendments are made to the Lords' amendments. These must go back to the Lords for approval, and the Lords may then amend the amendments to their own amendments. This process might continue for a very long time. Until both Houses agree over every amendment the Bill cannot pass. In Gladstone's last ministry the Employers' Liability Bill was 'bandied about' from House to House until the Government were forced to drop it.

Royal Assent

About once a fortnight, according to convenience, a Royal Commission is appointed to give the Royal Assent to Acts. 'The ceremony,' says Sir Courtenay Ilbert, 'dates from Plantagenet times, and takes place in the House of Lords. The King is represented by Lords' Commissioners, who sit in front of the throne, on a row of armchairs, arrayed in scarlet robes and little cocked hats. Sometimes a few peers in ordinary clothes are to be seen upon the benches, sometimes there are none. At the bar of the House stands the Speaker of the House of Commons, who has been summoned from that House. Behind him stand such Members of the House of Commons as have followed him through the lobbies. A Clerk of the House of Lords reads out, in a sonorous voice, the Commission which authorizes the assent to be given. The Clerk of the Crown at one side of the table reads out the title of each Bill. The Clerk of the Parliaments on the other side, making profound obeisances, pronounces the Norman-French formula by which the King's assent is signified: "Little Peddlington Electricity Supply Act. Le Roy le veult." Between the two voices six centuries lie.'[1]

1. *Parliament*, p. 75.

Bills founded upon Resolutions

In some cases, before a Bill is introduced, its main principles are discussed in Committee of the whole House. Resolutions embodying the main features of the Bill are agreed to and reported to the House. As soon as the House has agreed to the report of the Committee the Bill is ordered to be brought in.

Until 1938 this procedure had always to be followed in the case of what were then called 'Money Bills',[1] i.e. Bills which were mainly concerned with imposing a charge on the public revenue. The debate on the resolutions was inevitably a debate upon the main principles of the Bill, and therefore covered the same ground as the debate upon second reading. The same Members might make exactly the same speeches in Committee on the resolutions, in the House on report of the resolutions, and on second reading. For this reason a new Standing Order was made in 1938 (now S.O. No. 80), which allows Government Money Bills to begin their adventures in the same way as any other Public Bill, though difficulties still await them at a later stage, as will be explained shortly.

There are, however, other Bills where it is considered to be desirable to anticipate second reading debate at the very outset. Some Bills are so important that the Government is reluctant to cast them into final shape or issue them to the public until their main principles have been discussed. The Parliament Bill of 1910, which sought to alter the Constitution, was brought in upon resolutions, which occasioned lengthy and angry debate. The first resolution began as follows:

'That it is expedient that the House of Lords be disabled

1. These 'Money Bills' are not quite the same as the Money Bills which are defined in the Parliament Act (see below, p. 156) which deal *only* with money.

by Law from rejecting or amending a Money Bill, but that any such limitation by Law shall not be taken to diminish or qualify the existing rights and privileges of the House of Commons.'

This resolution was followed by two others of a similar drastic nature; all were adopted, and the Bill was brought in. Its second reading was successively deferred from week to week while negotiations went on between the two Houses, until the Bill was eventually killed by the prorogation. The Bill which eventually became the Parliament Act was introduced on a motion for leave.

Introduction on a Motion

The introduction of a Bill on a series of resolutions is not to be confused with the procedure of introducing a Bill upon a motion for leave to bring in a Bill, which has already been referred to, as an alternative to the customary presentation after notice. In this case the Member rises and makes his motion, and a general debate ensues upon the principles of the Bill.

If the motion is carried, the Speaker will say, 'Who will prepare and bring in the Bill?' To this the Member who has moved for leave will reply by reading out a list of the Members supporting the Bill, concluding with his own name. He then goes to the Bar: his name is called out by Mr Speaker, he advances to the Table of the House with three bows; and hands to the Clerk the 'dummy' Bill, a piece of paper endorsed with the title of the Bill, which the Clerk reads out to the House. A day will thereupon be appointed for second reading, just as in the case of a Bill presented upon notice.

The advantages and disadvantages of this procedure are similar to those attending the introduction of a Bill upon resolutions. There is an opportunity for a debate before first reading, which may be desirable, but may on the other hand merely anticipate the second reading debate. It may give rise to acrimonious debate before the Bill is even printed: an inauspicious beginning which befell the Protection of Life and Property (Ireland) Bill, and resulted in the famous long sitting mentioned in Chapter III, when the Irish Members kept a weary House in continuous Session for forty-one-and-a-half hours.

This procedure however does possess a peculiar advantage in the fact that a Bill brought in under it can under exceptional circumstances be introduced without the customary day's notice. It thus saves at least one day out of the time necessary to pass the Bill: and where there is extreme urgency it can be very useful. The Gold Standard Bill of 1932 and the Abdication Bill of 1936 were brought in on motions, partly for this reason.

Private Members' Bills

So far we have considered only the case of Bills promoted by the Government. In comparison with Members of the Government Private Members lie under a heavy disadvantage in promoting Bills as in other ways. It is the Government that draws up the programme of the day, and the programme of the Session: the Government which decides which Bills shall be taken, and when. The Bills which are set down by the Government are those Bills which it cannot afford not to put forward: it has no time for any others. Private Members who wish to promote Bills must hope for good fortune in the Sessional ballot for Fridays, and, if they wish their Bills to get through, for still greater good fortune thereafter. The time allotted for all stages of all Private Members' Bills is ten days in the Session.

The ballot for precedence on Fridays has already been described. The Members who are successful present their

Bills in the ordinary way (upon written notice) on the fourth day of the Session. They are then condemned to the heart-breaking task of trying to get the second reading of their Bill through in time. The majority of Private Members' Bills even though presented never get a chance of second reading: and many of those which do come up for second reading are defeated. Members promoting Private Members' Bills naturally try to win over the support of as many of their fellow-Members as possible: but even if a dozen Members can be collected at the right time to vote for them, there are almost certain to be at least a dozen Members sufficiently hostile to the Bill for one reason or another to vote against it. Every Bill is certain to injure someone in some way, and even if hostile Members do not want to vote against it they can 'talk it out'.

Apart from these rather restricting circumstances, Private Members' Bills follow exactly the course of Public Bills promoted by the Government.[1] Indeed some Bills which are ostensibly and visibly Private Members' Bills are really inspired by the Government Whips – this being one of the ways in which a harassed Government seeks to eke out its meagre ration of time.[2] Similarly, the Opposition Whips will have an agreement with some of their followers that if they are successful in the ballot they will take up a party Bill. And sometimes a Member who has a Bill to promote may have an arrangement with one or two of his friends who have no Bills to promote that if one of them happens to be successful in the ballot, and he is not, the successful Member will play the part of foster-parent to the orphan Bill.

1. They are, however, referred to a Standing Committee on which Private Members' Bills have precedence.
2. Also, perhaps, because Private Members who feel an urge to introduce legislation sometimes find it difficult to discover a subject for their legislation.

The Ten Minutes Rule

There is, however, one other way in which a Member desirous of promoting a Public Bill may proceed. He may bring in a Bill under the 'ten minutes rule'; which is the use of the old procedure of presenting a Bill upon a motion as described above, with the special restrictions set out in Standing Order No. 12. The picturesque ritual is as follows:

The Member will have handed in a motion for leave to introduce a Bill ('Mr A. – To move, that leave be given to introduce a Bill to, etc., etc.') upon the evening before he intends to move it. On Tuesday or Wednesday, after question time and before the commencement of public business proper, he will be called upon by Mr Speaker, and will make a short speech in favour of the Bill – a 'ten minute' speech. This will usually be followed by an equally brief speech from a Member or Members who are opposed to the Bill: and after that the Speaker will put the question that leave be given to bring in the Bill. If the motion is carried the Bill is presented and has its first reading: its future stages, unless the Government can be persuaded to give time, must take place at the time of unopposed business – just after 10.0 p.m. – but, if any Member objects to it then, it will be postponed indefinitely. In fact the prospects of getting such a Bill through all its stages without opposition are so remote that Members generally use the 'ten minute' procedure merely in order to ventilate the ideas which the Bill embodies. For this reason Captain Crookshank, speaking before the Select Committee on the Public Procedure of 1931, recommended the abolition of procedure altogether. His view, however, was not shared by other witnesses, and Standing Order No. 12 still remains in force. Although suspended during the war, it was revived in 1950, and was responsible for Bills such as that to allow cars to be parked unlighted in lighted streets.

Financial Resolutions

Up to 1938 every Bill whose subsidiary provisions entailed the expenditure of public money had to receive authorization by a financial resolution passed in a Committee of the whole House before the Committee stage of the Bill. Since 1938 this arrangement has been extended to all Government Bills proposing the expenditure of public money, including what were previously called 'Money Bills' – i.e. Bills whose *principal* provisions imposed a charge upon the public revenue. The latter Bills, as already mentioned, had previously to be introduced before *first reading* by a resolution in Committee of the whole House: and the object of transferring the taking of the resolution from before first reading to after second reading was to reduce the likelihood of a debate upon it – a debate which would be merely an anticipation of the debate upon second reading. Naturally, this change in the Standing Orders did not entirely rule out all possibility of a duplication of the second reading debate. The mere fact that the financial resolution was to be taken after second reading would not necessarily prevent Members from bringing up the same arguments twice, though the Chairman would not in fact be likely to allow a mere continuance of the second reading debate. But the theory was – and experience has shown it to be sound – that Members would be less likely to wish to speak upon a later stage of a Bill than upon its first appearance in the House.

Every such financial resolution must be set down upon the Order Paper. This is important, as we shall see. When the moment comes for it to be taken the Speaker inquires whether it has the King's consent; and a Minister will rise and indicate, by a bow or otherwise, that the King's recommendation has been given. The House then immediately resolves itself into Committee to consider the resolution.

Two important principles are here involved. The first is that any expenditure of public money must be considered in Committee – with all the freedom and informality of debate which that entails.[1] The other is that any proposed expenditure of public money must have the initial sanction of the King, acting on the advice of his responsible Ministers, before it is granted by the House of Commons.

The excellence of these two principles is undeniable. A full and free discussion in detail in the representative chamber of proposals to spend money is obviously desirable. Still more desirable is it that the executive Government should have the power to organize the expenditure of the public money for which it is itself responsible, and not be liable to sudden demands which would throw out of gear its whole financial programme. At the same time the observing of the latter principle makes the Government's control over legislation even more secure than the initial advantages of being the Government have already made it. Nearly all Public Bills include provisions requiring the expenditure of public money, and in each case there must be a financial resolution in a Committee of the whole House. This resolution is set out on the Order Paper for the day on which it is to be taken in Committee, and with it, in brackets, appear the words 'King's Recommendation to be signified.' The recommendation of the Crown is therefore to be signified, not to any resolution which might be come to in the course of debate, but to the resolution set out on the Order Paper.

It is out of order in the debate in Committee on the financial resolution to move any increase in the amount of

1. The historic reason for the Committee on a financial resolution was no doubt the distrust felt for the Speaker as an agent for the King, and the desire to get him out of the chair during the consideration of money resolutions. But see below, Chapters V and VI.

money to be allocated for the purpose of the Bill: since that would be taking from the Government its right to initiate proposals for expenditure of public money. Moreover the resolution generally specifies the particulars of the expenditure. It is accordingly out of order to move an increase of expenditure on any part of the proposals, even if on another part of the proposals a corresponding reduction is proposed, since it would be ruled to be voting public expenditure not formally authorized by the King. The only amendments to a financial resolution which may be discussed are amendments to reduce the amount voted, to omit items of expenditure, and to limit the objects of expenditure contemplated in the resolution. The possibility of really constructive amendment is thus restricted to an extent at which it might be said not to exist at all. Members may criticize, but their power of amendment is severely restricted. If it is desired to increase the amount of the grant the Government must be persuaded to withdraw the whole resolution and substitute another in its place, though once it is passed the Government is equally bound by it.[1]

This restriction applies to the whole course of the Bill through both Houses. No amendment can ever be proposed which would increase the total expenditure covered by the money resolution, or increase the expenditure on any particular item mentioned in the financial resolution where a limit is specified in the resolution. So that the more detail the Government put into the financial resolution, the greater is its control over the Bill in all its stages: and though since the report of the 1937 Committee upon financial resolutions the growing tendency to put the whole of the financial matter of the Bill into the resolution has been checked,

1. The Government can, of course, put down a further resolution imposing a greater charge. But see below, p. 190, on the matter.

there must always be a danger that the detail in the resolution will be a heavy restriction upon the course of the Bill.

The financial resolution thus gives a distinct advantage to the Government. It may be doubted whether it affords any other practical advantage whatever to anyone, except in so far as it opens an additional opportunity to Members for debating the Bill: and even this advantage is offset by the severe restrictions which the terms of the resolution impose upon the scope of amendment. Sir Ivor Jennings has suggested that the procedure could well be dispensed with. It is unlikely however that any Government will be willing to throw away such a useful weapon, or encourage anyone to remove it. There are the two financial principles which would have to be ignored if financial resolution in connexion with Bills were abolished. But for a detailed discussion of the matter the reader should consult Professor Jennings' *Parliament*, pages 249–64.

Parliament Act Procedure

It has already been mentioned that until both Houses agree upon every part of a Bill and upon every amendment to it, it cannot pass into law. What then happens when the Houses cannot agree? The Bill may be killed, as was the Education Bill of 1906. Now, on the other hand, if the Lords insist upon rejecting a Commons Bill, or drastically amending it, the Commons can invoke the Parliament Act of 1911, as amended in 1949, and pass it into law as sent up to the Lords, without their Lordships' consent.

For the purposes of this procedure there are two kinds of Bills: Money Bills, and other Bills. A Money Bill is a Bill which the Speaker of the House of Commons has certified to contain *only* proposals dealing with taxation, the Consolidated Fund, public money, the raising or repayment of loans by the State, and matters incidental to those subjects.[1] The word 'only' is important. The Government could not tack on to a Money Bill other provisions, and still obtain the Speaker's Certificate.

If a Money Bill is not passed within a month after it has been sent to the Lords, it may be presented to the King for Royal Assent as an Act, without the Lords' consent. The justification of this seemingly arbitrary procedure is that the Commons have a traditional right to deal with finance, to the exclusion of the other House; a claim which has been generally admitted since the earliest days of Parliament. The House of Lords rejected the Finance Bill of 1909 on the grounds that though its clauses were purely financial, the purpose of the Bill was to effect a deep social change, and so went beyond purely financial matters. The Government of the day retaliated by bringing in what became the Parliament Act, which gave what had previously been custom the force of law.

1. The definition as given in the Act is as follows:

'A Money Bill means a Public Bill which in the opinion of the Speaker of the House of Commons contains only provisions dealing with all or any of the following subjects, namely, the imposition, repeal, remission, alteration, or regulation of taxation; the imposition for the payment of debt or other financial purposes of charges on the Consolidated Fund, or on money provided by Parliament, or the variation or repeal of any such charges; supply; the appropriation, receipt, custody, issue or audit of accounts of public money; the raising or guarantee of any loan or the repayment thereof; or subordinate matters incidental to those subjects or any of them. In this subsection the expressions "taxation", "public money", and "loan" respectively do not include any taxation, money, or loan raised by local authorities or bodies for local purposes.'

Money Bills under the Parliament Act are not to be confused with 'Money Bills' which still require a series of resolutions in Committee of the whole House. In one case, all the provisions must be of a financial nature: in the other case, only the principal provisions of the Bill involve the spending of public money.

The procedure of the Parliament Act of 1911 applied to other Bills in the following way. If the Bill is passed by the Commons but rejected by the Lords three times (now, under the new Act, twice) in successive Sessions, it might be presented to the King as an Act immediately without obtaining the Lords' approval. In this case the justification is somewhat less complete. If the elected representatives of the people pass a measure three times in different Sessions it may be assumed that the measure has their very carefully considered approval; and in that case a hereditary, unrepresentative body ought not to be allowed to stand in the way of it. But in order to avoid any attempt on the part of a Government to abuse the Parliament Act procedure by proroguing Parliament twice or thrice in the year, and thus having several short Sessions in the space of a few months, it was laid down that in order to apply the procedure of the Act, at least two years (now, under the new Act, one year) must elapse between the original second reading of the Bill in the Commons, and the last third reading there.

How far did the procedure of the Parliament Act restrict the power of the Lords? The Labour Government of 1945–50 maintained that the last-mentioned provision (the lapse of two years), however desirable, did allow for considerable interference with legislation by a hostile House of Lords. It should be remembered that in 1947 the procedure of the Parliament Act had not been put into operation since 1918, partly because during the twenty-nine years which had elapsed since 1918 the Government in power had been almost continuously Conservative, and had therefore had a permanently favourable majority in the Lords. If the Lords had cared to be difficult, and recourse to the Parliament Act had become necessary, contentious Bills would have risked being held up for at least two years by a hostile upper House. For this reason the Government in 1947 presented

an amending Parliament Bill, the object of which was to
reduce the delay necessary for the operation of the Parliament Act from three Sessions to two Sessions, and from two
years to one year. Much controversy raged about this step,
not because of its nature, which was not generally opposed,
but because of its timing. It was alleged by the Opposition
that the sole purpose of proposing such a constitutional
change at such a critical moment in the nation's affairs was
to pacify certain members of the Cabinet who wished the
Bill to nationalize iron and steel to be introduced a Session
earlier than was eventually agreed upon, and feared that the
Lords would be able to kill the Bill if it were introduced
towards the end of the five years' duration of the Parliament.
Some colour was lent to this allegation by the fact that the
amending Bill included a retrospective clause applying the
reduced period to any Bill introduced before the new Parliament Bill was itself finally passed. The Bill was finally
passed in 1949, under the provisions of the old Parliament
Act, which it was designed to amend. The Iron and Steel
Act of the same Parliament threatened a resort to the same
weapon, but in the end the Lords allowed it to pass on the
understanding that the 'vesting date', which gave the time
at which the Bill came into operation, should be postponed.

There are, however, various complications. The precise
meaning of Section 2 of the Parliament Act of 1911 is
obscure, and it has never been decided (nor been clarified
by the amending Act) what would be the position if the
Lords, instead of rejecting a Bill the second time it was presented, merely adjourned the debate on second reading till
the end of the Session. Of course, when the end of the
Session came, the Bill would, according to the definition of
the Parliament Act, be deemed to be rejected. But what
then? It would then presumably be too late to submit the
Bill for Royal Assent, since that can be given only when

Parliament is sitting. Would the Bill have to be introduced and passed a third time in the next Session? Or could it merely be presented for Royal Assent without having passed through all its stages again? Would not the prorogation kill it, as in the case of other Bills? And in any case, what would happen supposing that there was no third Session, as indeed there would not be, if, as in this case, the Bill were originally presented in the life of the late Parliament? Would not the Bill be in danger of being lost? Could the Bill be 'popped into' the last Royal Commission of the Session?

Something like this did occur in 1914 over the Government of Ireland Bill, and the Established Church (Wales) Bill. In this case, however, the opposition of the Lords diminished very considerably at the last moment owing to the outbreak of war, and to the action of the Government in introducing a Bill to suspend the operation of the two offending Bills. In the end, by some process which to this day remains unexplained, the 'Act copies' of the two Bills were recovered from the possession of the Clerk of the Parliaments, and the Speaker, by a sort of *coup de main*, certified them as having complied with the provisions of the Parliament Act. They then received Royal Assent. Whether they were correctly certified is impossible to say since even the Speaker in question (Speaker Lowther) seems to have had grave doubts on the question (see Lord Ullswater, *A Speaker's Commentary*, p. 113).

It should be noticed that the original Parliament Act of 1911 was passed as a sort of substitute for a thorough reformation of the constitution of the House of Lords.[1]

1. The Preamble of the Parliament Act runs as follows:
'Whereas it is expedient that provision should be made for regulating the relations between the two Houses of Parliament. And whereas it is intended to substitute for the House of Lords as it at present exists a Second Chamber constituted on a popular instead of hereditary basis, but

Hybrid Bills

A word must be said about Hybrid Bills, since they have been of frequent occurrence in recent years. When a Public Bill appears *prima facie* to affect the private rights of individuals or corporate bodies, it is referred before second reading to the Examiners of Petitions for Private Bills. The Examiners are directed to see whether any of the Standing Orders which would, in the case of Private Bills, require notices to be given to parties affected, are applicable to the Bill. If they find they are not applicable, the Examiners report the fact to the House, and the Bill proceeds on its way. If the Standing Orders are applicable, the Examiners must report whether they have been complied with. In the case of a non-compliance, the Standing Orders Committee must sit upon the matter and decide whether the Standing Orders are to be dispensed with or not. If they decided that the Standing Orders should not be dispensed with, there would be little hope for the Bill. That, however, is unlikely to happen.

After second reading the Bill is referred to a small Select Committee, which meets to consider the Bill in the same way that a Private Bill group meets upon a Private Bill, with counsel and witnesses (except that in this case the principle of the Bill has already been decided by the House in the debate on second reading, and cannot therefore be impugned in the Committee). The Committee sits only to consider the complaints of individuals that their private rights have been affected by the Bill.

such substitution cannot immediately be brought into operation: and whereas provision will require hereafter to be made by Parliament in a measure effecting such substitution for limiting and defining the powers of the new Second Chamber, but it is expedient to make such provision as in this Act appears for restricting the existing power of the House of Lords.'

After the report of the Select Committee, the Bill is re-committed to a Committee of the whole House, and proceeds on its way as an ordinary Public Bill.

It will now be clear why the Bill is called a 'Hybrid Bill'. It partakes both of the nature and the procedure both of Public and of Private Bills.

It may well be asked whether, in fact, every Bill passed in Parliament does not in some way affect the private rights of individuals. Of course every Bill does affect the rights of private individuals. Only the normal Public Bill affects private individuals in definite and widely distributed classes. The Transport Bill of 1947, for instance, affected not single railway stock-holders, but all the holders of railway stock in Great Britain. The Coal Bill of 1946 affected not merely some mine-owners but all the mine-owners in Great Britain. These two Bills were, therefore, not Hybrid Bills. On the other hand, the Bank of England Bill of 1946 affected only the holders of shares in a particular concern – the Bank of England; and it was, therefore, ruled to be a Hybrid Bill. So also with the Cable and Wireless Bill of 1946 and the Parliament Square Improvement Bill of 1949. Obviously the distinction is not always very easy to draw, but it does exist, and it is of practical value, inasmuch as it would clearly have been impossible to send notices to all the innumerable people affected in various ways in, for instance, the process of railway nationalization. The distinction, in fact, is really a distinction between Public and Private Bills, which has been an accepted part of English legislation for hundreds of years. A Hybrid Bill is in most cases simply a sort of Private Bill promoted by the Government. The Government cannot promote a Private Bill, for the Crown cannot present petitions. It therefore must present a Hybrid Bill.

CHAPTER V

COMMITTEES

IT might be expected that in a great legislative assembly much of the work to be performed would devolve upon smaller bodies, chosen from the whole. This, to some extent, is so in the case of the House of Commons. Mention has already been made of the Committees which function in connexion with the Committee stage of Bills. Then there are the Committees – some of them Committees only in name – which deal with the scrutiny of national finance, and the numerous Committees which are set up from time to time to investigate important questions of the day. Nevertheless the amount of work which is thus delegated is a very small proportion of the whole. It is still a working principle of the British constitution that the House of Commons should itself handle at one stage or another all the matters which come before it. It is a principle which every year makes more difficult to maintain. 'It is confessed on all hands,' said Gladstone, ' – I do not speak of this Parliament, but of all – that there is no legislative assembly in the world that works itself so pitilessly, so relentlessly, as the British House of Commons.' If this was so in 1881, how much more so is it now? More and more voices are raised in complaint of the way in which Parliament is overworked. But the handing over of responsibility is such a dangerous step that up to now the principle has been to a large extent maintained.

The result is that the Committee system is not extensively developed in the House of Commons. In no country, perhaps, do Committees occupy such a small place in the operations of the representative assembly as in Great Britain. In some countries the legislative assembly has attempted, by means of its Committees, to take into its own hands the functions of the executive. In the United States there are Committees of Congress which formulate policy, and intervene in the actions of the Government. In the Third Republic of France a system of eleven bureaux, chosen by lot from the Chamber of Deputies, performed the same functions to an even greater extent. Nothing comparable to this exists or ever has existed in this country. Indeed such a conception is entirely foreign to the spirit of our Constitution. In this country the legislative assembly makes laws and criticizes policy in full Session: its Committees are only auxiliaries, the mere accessories of the legislative and critical machine.

The Cabinet, which might be cited as a very powerful joint Committee, is not really so at all. It sometimes includes men who are not Members of either House. Historically, it derives its origin rather from the Privy Council than from Parliament. And the Cabinet is not officially a Committee of either House. Neither House ever entrusts affairs into its keeping: it is chosen secretly, and appointed by one man, the leader of the majority, who does not consult the House about any of his nominees. The proceedings of the Cabinet are still a close secret, even to the House of Commons: it has no dealings with the House of Commons as a body: it has no organic connexion with it. In fact to describe the Cabinet as a Committee of either or both Houses of Parliament is strictly inaccurate. Neither House 'commits' anything to it. It allocates its functions to itself. So much must be said to make this point clear: otherwise the Cabinet is a subject outside the scope of this work. Those who are interested should certainly consult Sir Ivor Jennings' book *Cabinet Government*.

Committees, then, in the British House of Commons are not of overshadowing importance. There are nevertheless many important Committees, and many Committees which perform valuable work, which we must consider in their turn, though our consideration of committee work will be briefer than that of other aspects of the main subject.

It should be mentioned that there are a number of unofficial groups of M.P.s, large and small, which meet within the Palace of Westminster and are often called 'Parliamentary Committees' – 'the Parliamentary Scientific Committee,' for instance – although the term is not correctly applied here.[1] These bodies perform much good work. They act as a liaison between the Government and the ordinary Member. They keep a watchful eye upon the amenities and privileges of Private Members: to a certain extent, they supply an additional check upon the work of the Government. But such Committees have no very definite procedure, and no 'powers', apart from the power of individual persuasion. Strictly speaking they are not really Committees of the House any more than the Cabinet is: nothing is committed

1. Mr Speaker Clifton Brown has ruled thus (*Hansard*, 25 May 1943): 'The title "Parliamentary Committee" has a technical meaning and can be properly used only by a body appointed by one or both of the Houses of Parliament. Its use by bodies not so appointed is, as the hon. Member says, apt to mislead the public by suggesting that the body has an authority and powers which it does not in fact possess. It ought not to be impossible to find some other term to designate bodies, entirely or partly composed of Members of Parliament but not appointed by Parliament, which would sufficiently indicate their connexion with Parliament without giving rise to misconception. In some cases, "Private Members' Committee" would do; in others, "Parliamentary Group". I think the good sense and ingenuity of Members can be relied on to find a form of designation appropriate to each particular case, once the principle governing the use of the term "Parliamentary Committee" is pointed out.'

to them by the House. With them as with the Cabinet we have no particular concern here.

Committees of the Whole House

It is well known that the House of Commons has a double personality. There is the honourable House, with the Speaker in the Chair, and the mace honestly displayed upon the Table: but there is also the House sitting, 'in Committee' as it is called, released from Mr Speaker's paternal surveillance, with the mace surreptitiously concealed under the Table and an hon. Member who is known as the Chairman of Ways and Means controlling the proceedings from the accustomed chair of the Clerk of the House.

Many people find the name 'Committee of the whole House' puzzling. The generally accepted meaning of the word Committee is a portion of a more numerous body, whereas a Committee of the whole House consists of 624 out of the total 625 Members – the absent Member being, of course, Mr Speaker. But what the word 'Committee' originally meant was a person or body of persons to whom a matter was committed or entrusted for consideration and decision. In this sense, and in this sense only, the word 'Committee' is accurately applied to the House of Commons 'in Committee'.

The origin of Committees of the whole House has been traced back to the distrust felt in former times towards Mr Speaker, who, then a nominee of the King, and frequently his creature, was felt to be a spy upon the proceedings of the House, and a potential menace to the freedom of deliberation. Going into Committee was one means of getting rid of the Speaker. Another possible reason for the institution of the Committee of the whole House may have been the old habit of allowing any Members of the House who wished to attend the meetings of Select Committees, and even have voices therein: the logical result of which was to appoint the entire personnel of the House to the Committee.[1] But whatever may be the history of the Committee of the whole House, it has a *raison d'être* of practical importance. In Committee a Member may speak more than once to the same question, and this concession, however slight it may seem, is invaluable when discussing the details of legislation. In effect the presence or absence of the Speaker and the mace is useful as an immediate and constant reminder to Members of the nature of the discussion proceeding, and the limits upon debate.

Committees of the whole House meet for four distinct purposes. There is:

(1) The ordinary Committee of the whole House on a Bill;

(2) The Committee of the whole House on a Money Resolution;

(3) The Committee of Supply;

(4) The Committee of Ways and Means.

Enough has already been said in a preceding chapter[2] to make the use of the Committee of the whole House on a Bill, and on a financial resolution clear. The subject of the Committees of Supply and Ways and Means will be further discussed in the next chapter, on financial legislation. For the

1. Clarendon relates that after the visit of King Charles I to the House of Commons to seize the five Members, the House adjourned, having appointed a Committee to meet in the city, and 'all who came to have voices'. By this expedient the House was able to meet in full strength out of reach of the King's guard. The Committee proceedings had another advantage, in that 'they found it much easier to transact anything contrived and framed by such a Committee than originally offered and debated in either House before the mystery was understood by their proselytes, and when those, who too well understood it, did render their designs sometimes ineffectual'. *History of the Rebellion*, II, 179.

2. Chapter IV: 'How a Bill becomes an Act'.

moment it will be enough to say that the Committee of Supply sits to consider (at least in theory) the details of the money to be spent by the Government on the Army, the Navy, the Air Force, and the Civil Service – or, in technical language, to consider the supply to be afforded to His Majesty towards defraying the expenses of the public services. The Committee of Ways and Means sits in order to discuss the resolutions upon which the great Financial Bills of the year are founded, and to authorize the issue of money out of the Consolidated Fund (see below, Chapter VI).

How do Committees of the whole House work? How are they convened, and how do they end their sittings? The answer, in the case of the Committees of Ways and Means, and of Supply, is this: resolutions are passed at the beginning of each Session (generally immediately after an answer to the Address from the Throne has been agreed upon) that upon a certain future day the House will resolve itself into Committee of Supply, or of Ways and Means, as the case may be. After that, in the case of the Committee of Ways and Means, an item appears on the Order Paper, among the Orders of the Day, thus: 'Ways and Means: Committee': and upon this being read out, if the Order is not postponed, the Speaker at once leaves the Chair, followed by the Clerk of the House, the mace is placed underneath the Table, the Chairman of Ways and Means takes his seat in the Chair of the Clerk of the House – and immediately we are 'in Committee'. At the end of the debate, the Committee must hand the subject with which it has been dealing back to the House, so to speak. A motion is generally made 'That the Chairman do report progress, and ask leave to sit again.' This corresponds roughly to an adjournment motion in the House, and, like an adjournment motion is open to considerable debate, though the debate is now restricted to actual reasons for reporting progress or not reporting progress. The Committee, it will be noticed, asks leave to sit again. A Committee of the whole House is not set up permanently, but is a temporary body appointed from day to day: the idea, doubtless, being that the House must maintain full control over its creatures, and that the Committees should not be allowed to become separate Houses of Parliament.

When 'progress' has been carried, the Chairman leaves the Chair, the mace is replaced on the Table, the Speaker (or the Deputy Speaker) resumes the Chair, and the Chairman (or a Member deputizing for him) approaches the Chair and says 'I beg to report that the Committee have made progress in the matters referred to them, and ask leave to sit again.' The Speaker then enquires when the Committee is to sit again: one of the Government Whips answers him. The appointed day is then announced from the Chair and becomes an order of the House. Under modern conditions an air of unreality sometimes attends these proceedings. However, the distinction between the Committee and the House is preserved, and the hidden dangers which lurk beneath neglect of the forms of procedure are not invoked.

'Progress' is reported only when the Committee has not finished its work.[1] It may be, however, that the Committee end their day's work by agreeing to a resolution, or several resolutions. In this case the procedure is similar, except that the Chairman reports 'that the Committee have come to certain resolutions.' The Speaker then says 'report to be received – ?' and the Whips name a day. And if the Committee has already agreed to resolutions, and is in the course of considering another, the report is 'that the Committee have come to certain resolutions and that they also report progress and ask leave to sit again.'

The procedure in Committee of Supply is similar to that

1. If the proceedings be terminated by the 'hour of interruption', the Chairman leaves the Chair without question put, and reports progress.

in Ways and Means, except when one of the main groups of estimates (Army, Navy, Air and Civil Estimates) is to be considered for the first time in the year. In these cases the Speaker proposes the question 'That I do now leave the Chair,' and the House debates this or an amendment to this quite happily for the rest of the evening.

When it is desired to set up a Committee of the whole House upon a financial resolution it is the financial resolution which appears upon the Order Paper. The Order of the Day for the Committee will be read out and the Speaker will enquire whether the resolution has the King's recommendation. This assurance being given, the Speaker leaves the Chair and the mace disappears, as described above.

The case of a Committee of the whole House upon a Bill is simpler. If it is desired to send the Bill to a Committee of the whole House a motion to that effect must be moved immediately after the Bill is read a second time. Otherwise the Bill will go automatically to a Standing Committee (cases have been known where a Bill has gone to a Standing Committee by mistake). The Member in charge of the Bill will have to name a day for Committee, and on that day an item will appear on the Order Paper – 'Road Transport Lighting (Cycles) Bill [Lords] – Committee', upon which, when it is reached, the Speaker will leave the Chair without question put.

It has been found convenient to deal with the subject of Committees of the whole House here, although they are not Committees in the accepted sense of the word. The real Committees of the House of Commons are usually distinguished into four kinds:

(a) Standing Committees;
(b) Select Committees;
(c) Private Bill groups;
(d) Joint Committees.

Standing Committees

A Standing Committee is a miniature of the House itself – or rather, of a Committee of the whole House. It consists of from twenty to fifty Members, chosen by the Committee of Selection (of which more anon) so as to represent the relative strength of the different parties in the House. Its Chairman is armed with most of the authority of the Chairman of Ways and Means in the House, including the power to accept closure of debate, and power to select only certain amendments for consideration out of the total submitted (Kangaroo). He is appointed by the Speaker from a panel of Members chosen by the Committee of Selection – the Chairmen's Panel – which also supplies temporary Chairmen for the House itself.

Before the war from three to five ordinary Standing Committees were appointed every Session. Since 1945 more Standing Committees have been needed to deal with the increased volume of legislation, and as many as six Standing Committees have been appointed in a Session. Their function is to take over Bills for their Committee stage and thus to save the time which would be spent upon them if they were taken on the floor of the House. This sounds like a simple plan to solve an old difficulty; but of course there are 'snags'. Standing Committees sometimes prove unexpectedly argumentative; their deliberations upon a single Bill have been known to extend for several months, and the passage of the Bill to be accordingly delayed.[1] The duty of attending Standing Committees is onerous, especially for those Members

---

1. For this reason the 'Guillotine' procedure has, since the war, been extended to Standing Committees.

Attempts were made, in the Standing Committee on the Gas Bill of 1948, to hold up proceedings to a serious extent. The Committee sat from 26 February until 13 May, and even was forced to endure several all-night sittings.

who wish to take a full part in the work of the House the same day: their day's work in the Palace may well last for twelve hours, with only a short break between the rising of the Committee and the sitting of the House. It is therefore sometimes difficult to secure a quorum (now fifteen) of Members, and a Committee may have to adjourn abruptly more than once during the consideration of a single Bill. Then again, all the traditions of the House are towards taking as much work as possible in full Session: Members feel deeply the loss of the right to discuss a Bill in detail in Committee, and they will make up for it by talking at great length on report stage, so that in the end it may happen that no great amount of time is saved by sending a Bill upstairs. Nevertheless, in most cases, Standing Committees do save time, and it has now (since 1945) been decided to make use of them for many more Bills, although after the General Election in February 1950, it was found difficult to preserve the balance of parties in the small Standing Committees, and they were less used. It is widely believed that they are more efficient than the whole House when it comes to the details of legislation. It has even been suggested, particularly by Professor Ramsay Muir, that the system of Standing Committees could be extended to cover other fields of work. Supply, for instance, the estimates for the year, and many domestic matters could, it is suggested, be more easily and more competently dealt with by a smaller body than the full House of Commons. In fact the Scottish Estimates are now dealt with annually by the Scottish Standing Committee. But the argument is not by any means incontrovertible. For one thing the 625 Members who are supposed to make Committees of the whole House so unwieldy are never all present together. Generally in Committee of the whole House only a handful of really interested and alert Members are to be seen wrestling with the intricacies of legislation. For a full discussion of this problem the reader should consult the evidence published with the first report of the Select Committee on Procedure in 1945.

In addition to the normal Standing Committees, which are severally distinguished by the prosaic and business-like use of letters of the alphabet – Standing Committee A, Standing Committee B – there is another Standing Committee which has a more illuminating title: the Standing Committee on Scottish Bills. A concession to national aspirations, it is composed of all the Scottish Members in the House – seventy-one in number. Its task is to take the Committee stage of all Bills which refer exclusively to Scotland, and thus perform in a measure some of the functions of a Scottish Parliament. As the reader will observe, it is three times the size of the other Standing Committees.

The work of the Scottish Standing Committee is thus, to some extent at any rate, specialized. Otherwise, in the past, Bills have been referred to various Standing Committees on no particular principle, apart from a constant endeavour to allot them to the Committee which is most likely to be free to consider them first. It was originally intended, when the system of Standing Committees was instituted, that a particular Standing Committee should deal with Bills concerned with a definite class of subjects: e.g. trade, agriculture, etc. This has not been found practicable, owing to the irregular numbers of Bills of different classes.

Standing Committees meet in the mornings,[1] so as not to conflict with the sittings of the House. The mere alphabetical Committees have their rendezvous in one of the rooms on the Committee Floor of the Palace, particularly in the enormous Room 14, which is two Committee rooms

1. Before the war, generally at 11 a.m., since 1945, at 10.30 a.m., unless the Committee otherwise determine, but not between 1 p.m. and 3.30 p.m.

thrown into one – Sir Charles Barry not having contemplated the existence of such large Committees when he designed the building. The Scottish Standing Committee has its own home in the Grand Committee Room off Westminster Hall, a chamber which is also the cinema of the Palace.

The English Standing Committees usually consist of twenty[1] Members, including, as has already been mentioned, Members of all the political parties in about the proportion in which they stand in the House. To these are added about twenty 'specialists'[2] – i.e. Members specially interested in the subject under discussion, or specially qualified to discuss it. (Owing to the necessity of preserving the balance of political parties, not all these added Members can be specially qualified for the Bill under discussion – there are always some complaints.) 'Specialists' are also added to the Scottish Standing Committee in the same way.[3] The Committee of Selection, which has the unpopular task of nominating the Standing Committees in the first place, is also responsible for adding 'specialists' in respect of each Bill – not an easy task at any time, but infinitely more difficult in the case of the 'specialists' for the Scottish Committee, who must of course be English, Irish or Welsh Members, not normally interested in Scottish Bills. The Committee of Selection is also empowered to discharge Members from the Standing Committees, and substitute others in their place; and, except in the case of the most contentious Bills, it is generally possible for a Member who is particularly interested in a particular Bill – the Cotton Industry Bill, for instance – to get himself put on to the Committee for that Bill by approaching the Chairman of the Committee of

1. S.O. No. 58.
2. Not more than thirty – S.O. No. 58.
3. Not less than ten nor more than fifteen – S.O. No. 59.

Selection and by inducing someone of a similar political persuasion to step down and make room for him, if the personnel of the Committee has already been determined. Once the consideration of a Bill has begun, however, no changes in the constitution of the Committee may be made. In 1951 much difficulty began to be felt about the proportions of Members from the different parties to be appointed to the Standing Committees. Owing to the narrow majority of the Government in the election of 1950 it was impossible to make small Committees conform to the political pattern of the House; it would have involved adding fractional parts of Members to the Committee. After a defeat on a Bill in Standing Committee in 1951, the Committee of Selection increased the proportion of Government supporters in Standing Committees slightly. There was a 'row' in the House over this, but it was soon forgotten.

Procedure in a Standing Committee is the same as in Committee of the whole House, with certain important differences. Thus a Standing Committee cannot 'report progress and ask leave to sit again': it can only adjourn the meeting, or the debate.[1] The Chairman sits on a dais at the end of the room with the two clerks on his left and the Parliamentary Counsel and departmental experts on his right: while below him sit the official reporters – for Standing Committees have their *Hansard* too. The Members sit facing one another on long benches down the room, the Member in charge of the Bill being nearest the Chairman at the end of the bench on his right-hand side. There is an intimate, friendly atmosphere about the Committee: long orations are not popular.

At the beginning of its sittings a Standing Committee generally passes a resolution to meet on certain days of the

1. Adjournment motions may, of course, be moved at any time during the consideration of a Bill.

week (usually Tuesday and Thursday): otherwise a motion to adjourn to a fixed day will have to be made at the end of every sitting. The name of the Bill allotted to the Committee is then read out, and each clause debated separately, together with the amendments to it handed in beforehand.[1] At the end of the consideration of the Bill a motion must be made to report the Bill, as amended, or, without amendment, to the House. Failure to do this, or to adjourn to a particular day, would leave the Bill in a very peculiar state. Technically it would be lost; and it would have to be revived by a resolution of the House.[2] The actual report is handed in at the Table of the House on a printed form by one of the Clerks.

Select Committees

Standing Committees in their present form are a modern development. Sir Courtenay Ilbert has given credit for their invention to Sir Thomas Erskine May, who urged the adoption of a scheme of large committees for legislation, in an article in 1854;[3] and when he gave evidence before the Select Committee on Public Business, in 1878: though the prototype of the Standing Committee has also been found in the Grand Committees of the seventeenth century. Select Committees, however, are the result of an unbroken

1. Amendments to a Bill allotted to a Standing Committee should be handed in at the Table of the House, or in the Table Office. They will then be printed and circulated with the order paper. Manuscript amendments handed in during the sitting of the Committee, for parts of the Bill immediately under consideration, are not encouraged, though in order.

2. A Standing Committee must go through a Bill which is committed to it, and report it to the House. It may not lay it aside. A Standing Committee cannot 'report progress' – it can only adjourn to another day, or report the Bill to the House.

3. Contributed to the *Edinburgh Review*, January 1854.

tradition from the earliest periods.[1] 'Select Committee' merely means a Committee of Members selected from the total personnel of the House: but by long usage the name has come to be restricted to a body of special powers and privileges, to which the House has delegated its authority in a peculiar way. The name 'Select Committee' is vaguely associated in the public mind with the idea of an inquiry. Many people would find it hard to distinguish exactly between a Select Committee of the House of Commons and a Royal Commission. As a matter of fact the vulgar conception of a Select Committee is substantially correct. The main function of a Select Committee is to do the work for which the House itself is not fitted – the finding out the facts of a case; the examining of witnesses; the sifting of evidence; the drawing up of reasoned conclusions. A Select Committee has no executive powers.[2] It simply conducts its examination of the matter entrusted to it, and reports its findings to the House. It cannot ensure that any action will be taken to remedy any defects which it discovers, or to promote any advantage which it envisages. *A fortiori* it cannot give direct orders to have anything done which it thinks desirable. It will usually make recommendations to the House: but those recommendations may not be and frequently are not acted upon. For instance, the Select Committee on Equal Compensation reported in January 1943 that the compensation paid to men and women in respect of war injuries should be equal. The Government at first ignored the report, and was only forced to adopt its proposals by unceasing pressure – by

1. Anson, following Hallam, takes the view that the first Select Committee was appointed in 1689: Redlich traces the institution to a much earlier period.

2. Except for the Select Committee on Kitchen and Refreshment Rooms which exercises executive authority within the limited sphere of the dining rooms and kitchens of the House.

questions in the House, and damaging 'supplementaries': by
constant deputations and personal persuasion applied to
Ministers. Indeed it is possible, and even probable, that if
the Government had foreseen that the Committee would
come to such conclusions, and that so much support would
have been forthcoming for its attitude, they would have
resisted the 'setting up' motion more stubbornly. Whether
they could have refused the growing demand for it for much
longer is more doubtful.[1] Similarly the Government did not
accept the advice of the Select Committee on the MacManaway case in 1950.

We have seen how, during the passage of a Bill through a
Standing Committee, the Government has to keep a careful
watch over the activities of its followers, to prevent Government defeats on minor or even major points of the Bill.
Generally speaking, there is a Government Whip on every
Standing Committee, and for the most part it is possible, by
reason of the size of these Committees, to secure that
Government control of which so much has been said in the
last chapter. Human beings are always more manageable in
large numbers: their individual idiosyncrasies are sub-
merged in the mass of homogeneous party feeling. But the
small size of the ordinary Select Committee renders it almost
impervious to the authority of the party leaders. In spite of
the fact that the majority of the Members, and usually the
Chairmen, are Members of the Government party, the
effect of meeting in a small, compact body, round a table,
is disastrous to party solidarity; impartiality 'keeps breaking
through.' Consequently Select Committees are dreaded by
the Whips. They may lead to trouble or may come to con-

1. Here are some of the important Select Committees which have
functioned in the recent past: Marconi's Wireless Telegraph Company
Limited Agreement (1913); Sky-writing (1931–2); Musical Copyright
(1929–30).

clusions which are out of alignment with Government policy. They are one of the ways in which the House of Commons escapes from the bondage of Government authority. Even though they have no executive powers, their recommendations are public, and cannot be concealed. The report of the Committee is always a lever of which a dexterous Opposition can make very effective use. On the other hand a Government which has resisted a proposal until it has become impossible to resist it any longer, but has so compromised itself by resisting it that to give in would have the appearance of a complete *volte face*, sometimes will save its face by moving for a Select Committee on the matter, whose recommendations it can then gracefully accept.

Many people, including even experienced M.P.s, find the methods and procedure of Select Committees confusing and difficult to follow. This is mostly because a Select Committee is not a board meeting, or a debating society: its functions and therefore its conduct are entirely different. A brief account of the normal course of a Select Committee should suffice to explain this.

A matter is raised in the House – at question-time, or on the adjournment. Either Members are not satisfied with the Government's reply, or the Government itself feels that some matter ought to be looked into. At all events there is so much feeling aroused that the Government is forced to agree to the setting up of a Select Committee to investigate it. Any Member can move to appoint a Select Committee, by putting down a motion on the Order Paper. But here again, the Government can always block the 'setting-up' motion if it wishes, and if its majority is secure. It is therefore necessary for a Private Member either to win over the Government to consent, or – and the process is much the same in the end – to get heavy support for his proposal, before he can successfully move for a Select Committee. Motions to set up Select Committees are therefore generally put down by the Government, usually under pressure from groups of Private Members. The motion is generally taken at the time of unopposed business, just after the 'hour of interruption', late at night, and slips through without debate. If necessary, the Government will move to suspend the Standing Order regulating the rising of the House, so that the motion may get through, even with debate.[1] The motion thus proposed will contain the terms of reference of the new Committee, and the names of the Members who are to serve on it, including, by long-standing practice, Members of all parties. According to the rules of the House, not more than fifteen Members may be appointed to a Select Committee, without a special resolution. Larger Committees, had, before this rule was introduced (1836), been found to be very inconvenient.[2] To the order for their appointment will usually be added the magic words 'power to send for persons, papers and records', which give the Committee a right to summon any British subject (not being a peer or an M.P.); to make him cease his proper employment and come posting up to Westminster to give evidence before 'them' (a Select Committee usually adopts the regal plural).

The Committee being thus appointed, its senior member[3]

1. The motion may be opposed. Usually the purpose of opposition is to ventilate grievances arising out of the conduct of the Government, in the matters which form the terms of reference of the Committee, or out of the conduct of previous Committees. Thus in 1943 and 1944 Members opposed the setting up of the Kitchen Committee, complaining of the poor quality of the food served in the dining rooms under the control of the Committee.

2. The usual number of Members on Select Committees before 1836 was twenty-one – Redlich, op. cit. II, 213.

3. For this purpose, the senior Member is the Member who has been an M.P. the longest, adding together his various periods of service in the House.

fixes the time and place of the first meeting. A Select Committee may not meet outside the Palace of Westminster, or on a day when the House is not sitting, without special leave. This is because the Committee is only a creature of the House, and derives all its powers from the House. The rule is traditional, but its observance serves fittingly to emphasize this last-named fact. In a similar way the rule that a Select Committee may not appoint sub-Committees without the leave of the House serves to emphasize the fact that the House has delegated certain authoity to the Committee, and the Committee must not try to delegate that authority to someone else: *delegatus delegare non potest.*

The Committee will meet in one of the rooms on the 'Committee floor' of the Palace, and at its first meeting will elect a Chairman to preside over it until its work is done. Rival candidates may be proposed for this position: if necessary the clerk to the Committee must put the question formally, and call a division. The Chairman, when chosen, has none of the powers of the Chairman of a Standing Committee, and ought not, in so small a Committee, to need them. He cannot accept motions for the closure of debate; he cannot select amendments for discussion from among those offered. The Chairman of a Select Committee, like the Chairman of a Standing Committee, may vote only when the voices are equal; i.e. he has only a casting vote. He depends for his authority on the power of persuasion, and upon this also depends the expedition with which the Committee approaches its task. If he is unable to attend a meeting, the Committee must elect someone else to take his place *pro tem.*: they cannot appoint a deputy chairman: and the Chairman cannot appoint his own deputy.

At its first meeting the Committee will discuss the programme of their work, and decide what witnesses, if any to summon, and the day and time of future meetings. After all the evidence has been examined the Chairman will produce a draft report of the Committee's findings. This will be put to the meeting, and it is open to any member to propose an alternative draft report, or to propose amendments to the Chairman's draft report. The first question to be settled is whether the Chairman's draft report or some other member's draft report should be considered (or 'read a second time' in technical language). When this is agreed upon, the draft report is considered paragraph by paragraph, and amendments are debated in their proper places. It is out of order to consider amendments to parts of the report already agreed to: and, strictly speaking, if an amendment made to part of a report necessitates a consequential amendment to an earlier part of the report, the only way to effect it is to withdraw the whole report, and start again from the beginning with a new one. This rule should be strictly adhered to. A Committee can tie itself into inextricable knots if it attempts to tamper with parts of a report which have already been agreed to.

When the Committee have agreed to all the paragraphs of the report, the question is put, 'That the draft report (as amended) be the report of the Committee to the House.' A resolution is then generally passed to report the minutes of the evidence taken before the Committee to the House. This being done, the Committee's corporate existence is terminated. The clerk lays the report 'in dummy' on the Table of the House, and a copy, with the minutes of evidence, is sent off to the printers to be published as soon as possible.

The minutes of Select Committees are kept up by the clerk; and Members seldom see them until they are published, with the report and minutes of evidence.[1] Members

---

1. The 'Kitchen Committee' is an exception (the only one) to this rule: but then it is an executive body, not a Committee of Inquiry.

who are accustomed to the procedure of a board meeting or a county council sometimes express surprise at this, and wonder that the minutes are not read out at the beginning of each meeting, so that they can be certified by the Chairman as a correct record of what took place. The answer is that there is no need for it in the case of a Select Committee. A Select Committee is not (normally) an established executive authority but an *ad hoc* body set up to consider a particular case as it arises: its proceedings are not of immediate importance to anyone but itself: all that matters to the outside world is what it says in its report to the House. The need to check the record of the proceedings does not arise when that record is not, as in the case of a company meeting, the authority for outside action, but a list of members present, witnesses examined, and amendments moved to the report. Select Committee minutes are extremely brief, and to the point: they record not what is said, but what is done – by the Committee, not by the various members thereof. They are generally couched in the language peculiar to Parliament: elegant, dignified and (to the layman) unilluminating. What is very important is that they show when an alternative draft report has been moved to the Chairman's draft report. This is the only way in which a minority opinion in the Committee can be expressed. Otherwise the Committee is a solid entity, incapable of anything but unanimity. There is, therefore, no such thing as a minority report from a Select Committee.

After the Committee has reported, the minutes are sent to the printer with the report and the evidence by the Clerk to the Committee. This individual is one of the permanent staff of administrative rank which performs for the House of Commons what the Civil Service performs for the State. Besides keeping up the minutes, and conducting all the official correspondence of the Committee, he is expected to advise the Chairman on points of procedure. He must there-fore be well grounded in the study of parliamentary pro-cedure, and be able not to answer correctly every procedural problem as it arises – for that is beyond the wit of man – but to know where to look for the answer. He must remind the Chairman of things which chairmen tend to forget: the absence of a quorum, for instance.

Sessional Select Committees

There are, in addition to the various *ad hoc* Select Com-mittees which spring up in the course of the year, a number of perennial Select Committees which are almost permanent bodies. Some of these, like the Committee of Public Ac-counts[1] and the Standing Orders Committee,[2] are set up by Standing Order.

In addition to these there is the Committee of Privileges, the most authoritative Select Committee, composed of ten of the most experienced Members of the House, and usually including the Prime Minister or the Leader of the House, and the Attorney-General. To this body is referred most of the complaints of breaches of privilege mentioned in an earlier chapter. Its findings, however, are subject to the confirmation of the House. In one recent case – the case of a Member who was ultimately expelled from the House – the Report of the Committee of Privileges was in fact not accepted. As the Committee have to make recommenda-tions on the law of Parliament, and sometimes to express opinions on the conduct of erring Members, they have a responsible and judicial function. The Committee began to be appointed in the present form in 1902, in an effort to keep questions of Privilege off the floor of the House as much as possible.

Then there is a Select Committee on Statutory Instru-

1. S.O. No. 90.   2. S.O. (Private Business) 103.

ments. A vast number of rules and regulations (now, under an Act of 1946, called 'Statutory Instruments') made in the course of the year are made by Ministers of the Crown under the powers given them by some parent Act. Thus for instance all the regulations governing the sale and price of controlled commodities – food and clothing and so on – are made under Acts such as the Supplies and Services Acts of 1945–51, or the Goods and Services (Price Control) Act, 1941. Some Statutory Instruments do not need to be laid before Parliament: others must be laid before Parliament, but Parliament is given no right to debate them. In some cases the Order is 'laid' on the Table of the House, and, unless some Member moves a 'prayer' to annul it, during the period of forty sitting days during which it is vulnerable, it automatically becomes law without further difficulty. In other cases an *affirmative resolution* is required: the House must pass a resolution to approve the Order: but this usually takes only a few moments at the end of a sitting.

Statutory Instruments which are laid before Parliament and are subject to proceedings in either House, i.e., less than half of the 2,000 or so made each year, are now referred to a Select Committee, whose duty it is to scrutinize them under very restricted terms of reference, for unusual or unexpected use of powers conferred by the Act, need of elucidation, etc. The Committee have the assistance of the Speaker's Counsel, who lends his vast experience of the statutes to their deliberations. But it may be wondered how with even so great a legal luminary alone to help them the Committee can adequately deal with such a vast body of delegated legislation.

The Committee report such Orders as seem to need special attention to the House: they cannot report detailed opinions on them.

There is the Select Committee on Kitchen and Refreshment Rooms, a Committee which is set up to administer the Refreshment Department of the House of Commons, and therefore presents the curious anomaly of a Select Committee with administrative duties. There is also the Select Committee on Publications and Debates Reports, whose order of reference empowers it to assist Mr Speaker in arrangements for the reporting and publishing of debates, and the arrangement of the Order Paper, and also to investigate the expenditure on stationery and printing for the House and the public services. This is the Committee which deals with complaints about *Hansard*, and (less frequently) about the waste of paper by Government departments. It has been held, and with reason, that both of these Committees might disappear, and hand over their functions to less formal bodies. Then there is the Committee on Public Petitions, whose duty it is 'to classify and prepare an abstract of' the petitions presented to the House in each Session: but as these seldom number above half a dozen, its duties are not heavy.[1]

Joint Committees

Occasionally, when a matter has aroused interest in both Houses, a Joint Committee of Lords and Commons is set up to investigate it. From the point of view of the House of Commons, a Joint Committee is simply a Select Committee deputed to meet a Select Committee of the Lords. The Commons members of the Committee therefore form quite a distinct body, with powers conferred on them and a quorum fixed for them by their own House, and the duty of making their report to it. The Committee cannot proceed unless a quorum of Commons members (or, for that matter,

1. The Select Committee on Estimates, and the Select Committee on National Expenditure, which also come under this heading, will be dealt with in the chapter on Financial Legislation.

a quorum of Lords) is present. It is doubtful whether it can proceed to do anything which it is not specifically empowered to do, by both Houses. Joint Committees are, like Standing Committees, a rather recent development, and their powers and procedure are a little uncertain. Their setting up is dependent upon a lengthy exchange of messages between the two Houses, and though their actual procedure, which follows the rules of the House of Lords, is more informal than that of the ordinary Commons' Select Committee, the fact that they are of two distinct elements sometimes entails a great deal of formal difficulties, especially in reporting. For this reason, and others, Joint Committees are not a common feature of the parliamentary landscape. They are generally used for the Committee stage of purely uncontentious Bills, such as Consolidation Bills. The detailed Committee work in each House is thus telescoped; for although the Bills have to be recommitted to a Committee of the whole House in each House this is a pure formality, and occupies only a few minutes. Nevertheless, as already indicated, matters of inquiry are sometimes committed to Joint Committees. Perhaps the most famous case is that of the Joint Committee on Indian Constitutional Reform in 1933. A Joint Committee was set up to enquire into the problem of closer unity in the territory of East Africa in 1931, and another in 1935–6 to decide whether the measurement of gas should be in therms rather than cubic feet.

Private Bill Groups

Little need be said here about the Committees which are set up to deal with the Committee stage of Private Bills. They are nominated by the Committee of Selection, and follow the procedure of Select Committees, with modifications. Four Members compose a Private Bill group, including the Chairman, who is designated by the Committee of

Selection, and who has both a vote and a casting vote, unlike the Chairman of an ordinary Select Committee. The subject can be more conveniently discussed in the section on Private Legislation.

With this brief résumé we may leave the subject of Committees, which is, after all, only a lesser transept of the great procedural edifice, and turn to parts more important structurally.

CHAPTER VI

FINANCIAL PROCEDURE

ON first encounter the financial procedure of the House of Commons seems immensely complicated. Many an honest Member of Parliament has only the vaguest idea of the general order of financial procedure, and even Ministers have been found at a loss to explain the difference between a resolution in Supply and a resolution in Ways and Means. Yet the outlines of public finance as far as Parliament is concerned are extremely simple – too simple, in fact, to meet the approval of experienced statisticians, as we shall see later. Once the distinction between Supply and Ways and Means is grasped, once it has been realized that for a large part of the Session the House of Commons is actually voting money for two distinct financial years, there should be no difficulty in following the rest of the procedure.

Underlying all the financial procedure of the House are certain ancient maxims or rules, some of them the prize of centuries of struggle with the Crown. Briefly, they are:

(1) The granting of public money, and the imposing of taxation, is the function of Parliament, not of the King or the Government.

(2) Redress of grievances, or at least a full and public representation of grievances, must precede any grant of public money.

(3) The process of granting public money and imposing taxation must begin in, and be finally determined by, the House of Commons. The House of Lords has little or nothing to do with finance.

(4) All granting of public money, and all imposing of taxation, must begin in a Committee of the Whole House. It must then be agreed to by the House itself ('report') and finally be incorporated in an Act of Parliament.

(5) All granting of public money, and all imposing of taxation, must receive initial approval from the Crown (King's Recommendation), expressed by, and on the advice of, one of its responsible Ministers.

One word about these maxims. They are all very historical and entitled to the reverence which we accord to the very historical, but their importance is historical and constitutional rather than financial. Rule (1) was the bone of contention between King and Parliament for many centuries, ending in the civil war between Charles I and Parliament. Undoubtedly the Estimates for the Civil Service and the Forces and the Budget proposals for taxation are laid before Parliament in the first place; but they are laid before Parliament as drafted by the Government's Treasury Officials: and, since the Government controls the majority of votes in the House of Commons, those Estimates and Budget proposals will, in nine cases out of ten, receive approval in the form in which they were laid. Then again, it has been found necessary to maintain rule (5), since otherwise the Government's whole financial policy might be thrown out of gear by capricious or irresponsible demands for money by unofficial Members of Parliament, under pressure from constituents or patrons but obviously the existence of a sole right to initiate financial provision on the part of the Crown must seriously diminish the control which Parliament claims over the granting of public money. So much is this so that an eminent financial authority has described the position as 'Government authority' pure and simple. That of course is true only, here as elsewhere, to the extent to which the Government maintains the voting majority in the House of Commons. Moreover it is still possible even for a minority to press its point of view so strongly in the House that the Government will withdraw or revise its Estimates.

Finally, it must be realized that rule (2) – redress of grievances before the granting of Supply – has now been construed to sanction wide debates on all sorts of subjects on the motion to approve the various Estimates. Only in the case of Supplementary Estimates is the debate narrowly confined to the financial matters before the House, or the Committee. In fact, in most cases the Estimate is only a peg on which to hang a debate on policy of the widest possible scope.

We may now consider briefly the different elements of financial machinery in the Commons.

1. *The Consolidated Fund.* The whole system of national finance depends on the Consolidated Fund. Before 1787, when Pitt inaugurated this fund, it was customary to pay for the various public services with the produce of specific taxes especially levied for each particular purpose: and though to some extent machinery had been established for aggregating revenue and expenditure, the system of national finance was still complicated and inefficient. By the Act of 1787 which established the Consolidated Fund, all revenue was collected into one fund, and all expenditure provided out of that fund.

The Consolidated Fund has been spoken of as the great reservoir into which all the revenues of the kingdom are poured and out of which all the money required for public expenditure is drawn. It is not of course, contained in a great vault or strong-room at the Treasury. *Physically* speaking it has no existence. When we begin to speak of hundreds of millions of pounds we are talking, not about real money – gold bars, pound notes, shillings and pennies – but about figures in account books. So it is just an account, lodged at the Bank of England; and money is paid out from it into the account of the Paymaster-General only when, and to the amount, authorized by Parliament. The Paymaster-General then pays out the money from time to time to the various departments as it is needed – though here again, of course, the paying is simply a matter of transferring figures from one account to the other.

2. *The Session and the Financial Year.* The money which is paid out of the Consolidated Fund by order of Parliament is paid out only for one financial year; and the financial year is a completely closed period. Every department is allowed a sum of money for one financial year; it may not apply any part of the sum to the expenses of another financial year. Surpluses must be surrendered at the end of the year: deficits must be accounted for, if necessary, with sweat and tears. This necessity of budgeting for each financial year separately governs not merely the whole of the financial procedure of the House, as we shall see, but the whole course of the Session as well.

As the parliamentary Session usually begins in autumn, and the financial year always begins on 1 April, the two periods overlap by about six months, and this is often a cause of confusion to students. So the reader may find the following diagram helpful when we come in the following pages to consider the course of the Session in finance.

The right-hand side of the two parallel lines indicates the succession of financial years. The left-hand side shows the succession of parliamentary Sessions, together with the financial business proper to each period of the Session. It will be seen that the end of the financial year cuts each

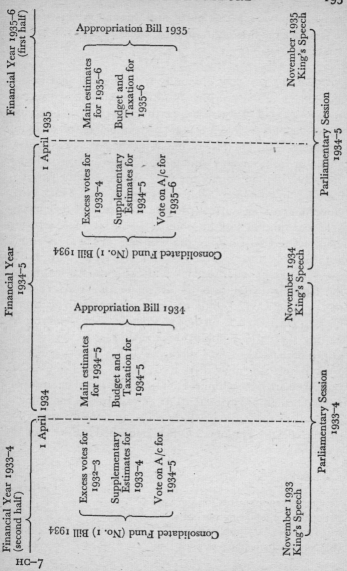

Session into two separate parts, and we shall, when we come to consider the Session in finance, consider it in two appropriate sections.

3. *The Estimates*. Now obviously it is essential that before Parliament is asked to provide any money for the public services it should know just how much is needed, and what it is needed for. Just as a private person, before he entrusts a contractor with the duty of making extensive alterations to his house, asks for an estimate of the possible cost, Parliament, before it authorizes the year's work, asks the Government for an estimate of what it is going to cost. So the great Government departments prepare Estimates of their probable expenditure for the coming financial year, and lay them before Parliament in the February of each year. They are in a prescribed form, consisting of five main divisions – the Army Estimates, the Navy Estimates, the Air Estimates, the Civil Estimates, and the Revenue Department's Estimates. The Civil Estimates are further subdivided into Classes, each Class is further subdivided into Votes, representing the various public departments (e.g. the Foreign Office is Class II, Vote i of the Civil Estimates), and each Vote is further subdivided into Items. The Estimates as published are huge volumes containing a mass of information for the benefit of Parliament. As an example of the amount of detail in the Estimates here is the account for paper for the use of H.M. Stationery Office, published in the Estimates of 1945:

E. – PAPER:

	1945	1944
Estimated requirements for the year of paper for the following purposes:		
(a) Parliamentary publications	14,000	9,000
(b) Non-Parliamentary publications	46,000	41,000

(c)	Printing and writing	1,040,000	1,040,000
(d)	Envelopes	135,000	135,000
(e)	Drawing and photographic	125,000	125,000
(f)	Blotting, wrapping and miscellaneous	120,000	120,000
(g)	Supplies and services on repayment terms (*see* Subhead M – Appropriations in Aid)	130,000	145,000
	Total	£1,610,000	£1,615,000

It will be noticed that the estimate for the previous year is here, as always, included in a separate column, for purposes of comparison.

It is the approval of these Estimates which constitutes the great bulk of the financial work of every Session.

4. *Supplementary Estimates.* It may happen (and generally does happen) that from one cause or another the Estimate which has thus been prepared of the probable expenses of a department for the year falls short of the total which is actually required. If the officers of the department realize that they have under-estimated their needs before the financial year has actually ended (31 March), they come and ask Parliament for more money. Parliament naturally wants to know how much more money is wanted and what it is wanted for, and so the departments prepare *supplementary* estimates of the additional money required: and these have to be dealt with as soon as possible, so as to avoid a deficit at the end of the financial year.

5. *Votes on Account.* Now if, as we have seen, the consideration of the Estimates supplies the main financial business during the whole parliamentary Session, something has to

be done to keep the departments supplied with money until the Estimates are approved. The financial year begins in April: the Estimates are not usually passed until the end of July. So the departments of the Civil Service draw up provisional estimates of the money they are likely to require during those four months. These estimates are presented to Parliament as a *Vote on Account*, and considered as expeditiously as possible. Thus, for instance, on 3 March 1936 a sum of £165,890,000 was voted on account to meet the needs of the Civil Service during the first few months of the financial year 1936–37.

In the case of the Service departments – (Army, Navy, and Air Force) – no Vote on Account is usually necessary. Its place is taken by a rather odd expedient. At the head of the Army, the Navy, and the Air Force Estimates the first item always is, 'Pay, etc., of Officers and Men.' This item is brought up, debated and (invariably) passed before the beginning of the financial year: and by an arrangement known as *virement* the accounting officers of the Services are permitted to apply the money which has been granted to them only for pay to supply all the other needs of the Services for the months which elapse before the full estimates are agreed upon. Naturally, this would not be possible except for the fact that the pay of personnel is one of the biggest items of Service expenditure. If it is not sufficient by itself, other items are taken as well. For instance, on 15 March 1935, the following sums were voted to supply the expenses of the Navy for the first few months of the year 1935–6:

£12,868,000 (Wages, etc., of Officers and Men of the Royal Navy and Royal Marines, and Civilians employed on Fleet Services).

£2,209,750 (Works, Buildings, and Repairs at Home and Abroad).

£3,281,400 (Victualling and Clothing for the Navy).

£3,200,000 (Non-Effective Services (Naval and Marine) – Officers).[1]

6. *Excess Votes*. Sometimes it happens that a deficit between the estimate and the expenditure of a department is not discovered until the end of the financial year in which it is incurred. It is then too late to present a supplementary estimate, and the department must draw upon the Civil Contingencies Fund to make good the deficit. An *excess vote* is then passed to legalize the overdraft of the department. Parliament pardons the mistakes of the officials, and 'tells them not to do it again.'

Excess votes must be clearly distinguished from supplementary estimates. A supplementary estimate is made when a department realizes, before the end of the financial year, that it has under-estimated its requirements. An excess vote arises when a department finds out after the end of a financial year that it has incurred a deficit.

Excess votes are naturally few and far between, since they amount to a confession of incompetent estimating or bad accountancy on the part of the department concerned. Most of them involve trifling sums – £50 or £100. There was, however, an excess vote of £63,200 4s. 7d. in 1943 over the newly-instituted supplementary pensions, the provision for which turned out to be hopelessly inadequate. In this case the cause was not so much incompetent estimating, as the sheer impossibility of arriving at any reliable basis for estimating possible claims.

7. *Votes of Credit*. Excess votes, again, must not be confused with votes of credit – large lump sums granted for unspecified purposes in time of emergency, particularly in war-time. For instance, in May 1943 the House granted a Vote of

1. Occasionally, where the Session is interrupted by a dissolution, a Vote on Account is taken for the armed forces.

Credit of £1,000,000,000 to the Government to carry on the war. Going back half a century we find Gladstone, in 1885, asking for a Vote of Credit of £11,000,000 to prepare for a threatened war with Russia over Afghanistan, and thereby incurring considerable criticism from those who disliked his pacifist attitude in the Sudan. Going back still further to 1797 we find Pitt bitterly attacked by Fox for applying £1,200,000 from a vote of credit for a loan to Russia, without the express sanction of Parliament; and Pitt replying that the vote of credit was granted 'to enable His Majesty to take such measures as the urgency of affairs might require.' Most of the expense of the late war was met from various votes of credit: the actual estimates presented being mostly token sums. It will be obvious that, as the uses to which vote of credit money may be put are not exactly specified, it is not a desirable way of providing money in peace-time.

8. *Supply and Ways and Means.* The authorizing of these various grants which have been mentioned takes place in the first instance in the two Committees of Supply and Ways and Means.

The function of the Committee of Supply is to sanction expenditure on the Army, the Navy, the Air Force, and the Civil Services – that is, to sanction all expenditure of public money which is not (a) otherwise sanctioned by an Act of the same Session, or (b) paid directly out of the Consolidated Fund.[1] It is the Committee of Supply which considers and approves the Estimates. The Estimates are con-

---

1. Certain high officials are paid directly out of the Consolidated Fund – e.g. Judges, the Speaker, the Comptroller and Auditor General. This means that their salary has not to be voted annually and they are thus supposed to be raised above political considerations. Interest on the National Debt is also paid directly out of the Consolidated Fund, and is by far the largest of the amounts so paid.

sidered in Committee, and not in the House, for the two main reasons already stated – (1) historical – the former necessity of getting rid of the Speaker when the voting of money to the King was under consideration, (2) practical – the necessity of having a somewhat less formal style of debate when dealing with the intricacies of financial legislation. But as has already been hinted, neither of these reasons is very cogent nowadays. The debates in Supply on the Estimates are very seldom devoted to properly financial matters. They are almost invariably general debates on the policy of the Government in relation to the services provided for: and therefore the technical freedom of Committee procedure is ultimately not of practical importance.

Formerly the passing of the various votes in Supply was one of the biggest headaches of the Government of the day. To hold up the vote for as long as possible, to endanger the Government's source of income, was a recognized tactic, nay, a right, of the Opposition. But now all that is changed. Nowadays, by an extension of the 'guillotine' procedure, which has been described above, twenty-six whole days (formerly twenty) must under the Standing Order be allotted each year for the consideration of the Estimates, for the consideration of the Votes on Account in Committee of Supply, and for the consideration of the Report of the Committee to the House. At the end of the twenty-six days (or rather, as will be seen, at the end of the twenty-fifth day) all the Votes which have not yet been passed must be put and agreed to or negatived, without any further debate. But although no further debate is permitted the House can still divide on the Votes which have not yet been passed (and there are generally a large number). It was at one time the normal practice of the opposition to force a division on each class of the Estimates. Vast sums of money were approved in this way, every Session, without any discussion at all in the chamber.

More recently the habit of dividing on outstanding Votes has been abandoned, but it is still the case that large portions of the Estimates are authorized without discussion at the end of the twenty-six allotted days. In view of the complexity of the Estimates it is difficult to see how it could be otherwise. The twenty-six days must occur before 5 August.

The Committee of Ways and Means has two functions to perform. It authorizes the Government to raise money to supply the needs of the public services. It considers and approves all taxes which are either (a) being applied for the first time, or (b) being increased for the ensuing year (or if their incidence is being altered), or (c) are subject to annual revision under the terms of the Act by which they were originally applied. In this way the Committee of Ways and Means is concerned with paying money into the Consolidated Fund.

The second duty which the Committee of Ways and Means has to perform is rather confusing to the layman. The Committee has to authorize the payment out of the Consolidated Fund of the moneys which are required for the public services. The reader will object that this has already been done in great detail by the Committee of Supply. Technically, however, this is not so. The Committee of Supply approves the uses to which the money may be put: it approves the spending of it. The actual issue of the money from the Exchequer is controlled by the Committee of Ways and Means. It is perhaps a rather fine distinction, and, of course, as no money is actually handled in any of these transactions, its importance is more theoretical than practical. This process actually occupies very little time.

THE COURSE OF THE FINANCIAL YEAR

(a) *Before* 1 *April*

Let us now trace the story of the financial procedure of the House step by step from the beginning of the Session. The starting point is the passage in the King's Speech from the Throne at the State Opening of Parliament, when His Majesty pauses and addresses the House of Commons alone:

> *Members of the House of Commons:*
> The Estimates for the Public Service will be laid before you.

It is in answer to this that the House of Commons, as soon as it has agreed upon the address in reply to the King's Speech, proceeds to set up the Committees of Supply and Ways and Means. Thereafter the first piece of financial work to be performed is usually the consideration of the supplementary estimates for the current year, and also of excess votes, if there are any, on previous years.

The Session usually begins in autumn. The first sitting of the Committee of Supply may be in November, or on the other hand may not occur until January. At all events, at this meeting the supplementary estimates for the financial year then proceeding – i.e. the year for which Estimates have already been voted in the Session which has just closed – will be dealt with. For instance, in Session 1944–45 the Committee of Supply first sat on 13 December 1944 to consider supplementary estimates for the financial year beginning 1 April 1944. (If this sounds complicated the reader should refer again to the diagram on page 193.) On such occasions 'Committee of Supply' stands on the Order Paper as an Order of the Day and upon this Order being read the House automatically resolves itself into Committee of Supply. There is in this case no question of debate on going into Supply – no 'getting the Speaker out of the Chair' – all that is reserved for a later stage, when there is less urgency. Moreover the debate in Committee of Supply on a supplementary estimate is unlike the debate on the main Estimates in that it is confined to the subject of the sums being voted, and is therefore a more truly financial debate than most of the Supply debates. It is true that the sums voted were formerly rather small and the objects for which they were voted insignificant – since they are, in effect, the result of mistakes in estimating, or of sudden changes of policy. Mr Winston Churchill has spoken of them as the most worthless of any that he had known in his career. 'The House,' he told the Committee on Procedure in 1931, 'makes a great fuss about some Embassy that has been built somewhere, or it is angry because a bathroom has been put in the Lord Chancellor's house, and so on, and four or five days are often consumed in discussing it; those are precious days.' On the other hand, on 17 February, 1949, the Committee of Supply had to authorize an extra £52,800,000 for the National Health Service, and on 23 March, 1950, an extra £89,400,000 for the same purpose, and £13,880,400 for the Ministry of Food. Recent conditions have made accurate estimating of needs very difficult. The supplementary estimates were not included in the old twenty allotted Supply days, so that there was no check upon the time spent on them, however insignificant they might be.

Meanwhile (probably in February), the main Estimates will have been presented to Parliament, and referred to the Committee of Supply, and the Committee will be able to proceed with its next business, namely to pass enough of the Service Estimates to keep the Army, the Navy, and the Air Force in being from the beginning of the coming financial year (1 April) until the whole of the Estimates are finally dealt with. This may be said to be 'where the fun begins'.

For, as we have seen, before granting money to the executive the subject is entitled to have his grievances remedied, or at any rate listened to: and hence the modern practice that on first going into Committee of Supply upon the Army Estimates, upon the Navy Estimates, upon the Air Estimates, and upon the Civil Estimates there shall be debate upon whether the Speaker shall leave the Chair (i.e. whether the House shall resolve itself into Committee). The debates take place upon the question 'That the Speaker do now leave the Chair,' – and upon amendments to this motion, moved by Members who have secured the right as a result of the Sessional ballot, in the manner described in Chapter III. The subject of each amendment must be relative to the Estimates which are under consideration, and the debate on each amendment must be relative to the subject of the amendment. For instance, on first going into Committee on the Army Estimates, 1945, a Member moved the following amendment:

That this House is of opinion that, in view of the strong feeling that exists in the Army on the question of demobilization and re-employment, an advisory council be set up, composed of five officers and ten other ranks, and that all measures necessary be taken to ensure that all men due for demobilization are so trained that they can be fitted into useful employment with the minimum of delay.

And on first going into Committee on the Naval Estimates, 1943, another gallant Member moved an amendment:

That this House desires to record its admiration of the part played by the members of the Women's Royal Naval Service in the present conflict and to express the opinion that a still further extension of their activities should be considered.

And so on. At length each amendment is withdrawn or

defeated, the question is put and agreed to, and the Speaker leaves the Chair.[1]

The debate in Committee on the Service Estimates is sometimes just as long and discursive as the debate on getting the Speaker out of the Chair. It usually turns, not at this stage upon the money being voted, but upon the number of officers and men for the Service ('Vote A'), which is set out at the head of the estimate. For instance, on 17 March 1936 when the House was in Committee on the Air Estimates, a Member moved to reduce the number of R.A.F. personnel from 50,000 to 45,000 in order to debate the condition of the country's air defences. It was not that the Member felt any antagonism towards the R.A.F.: still less that he really wanted to reduce the number of pilots and aircraftmen in the Service: on the contrary, he professed himself to be extremely worried (not without reason, as it afterwards appeared) about the inadequacy of our air fleet. There was in fact nothing else that he could do to express his feelings. He could not move to increase the number of men on the books of the force: for this would have entailed extra expenditure, which, as we have seen, only the Crown may sanction. Still less, of course, could he move to increase the actual estimate. All he could do was to move to reduce the number of men. It cannot be too strongly stated that this is the case with this and with all the Service estimates. The only way of protesting about their inadequacy is to move to reduce them still further. The amendment, of course, is ultimately withdrawn or negatived – if it were not, the Government would most likely feel obliged to resign – and it serves, once again, only as a peg to hang the debate on. It

1. Very occasionally an amendment is carried. This could only happen, of course, where there was a Government with a small majority, or which was otherwise weak. The main question could, of course, be put again on a subsequent day.

is a process perfectly well understood inside the House of Commons. Outside it, unfortunately, where the precise nature of financial procedure is not understood, attempts have been made to make political capital out of it. Once again, then, this process of moving to reduce votes in Supply has no financial significance *whatever*.

Another curious point about procedure in Supply is the way the amendments are put. In the case just cited, the Member moved to reduce the total strength of the force from 50,000 to 45,000 men (such was the diminutive size of our Air Force in those far-off days). The motion was 'That a number of Air Forces, not exceeding 50,000, all ranks, be maintained for the service of the United Kingdom at Home and Abroad, excluding those serving in India (other than Aden) during the year ending on the 31st day of March 1937' and the reader, bearing in mind what has been said in Chapter II, will naturally suppose that the question put on the amendment would be 'That the word "50,000" stand part of the question' – to be followed by another question, 'That the word "45,000" be there inserted ' Not at all: the question put is just this: 'That a number, not exceeding 45,000 all ranks, be maintained for the said service.' In other words, the original question is simply put again, with the new figure in place of the old. And this is true of *all* amendments in Supply (whether to Votes on Account, or to the main estimates), most of which, of course, are to the actual figures of money.

The reason for this departure from the normal, the excellent practice of the House with regard to amendments has been variously stated. May (2nd Edition, p. 421) suggests that the moving of amendments in place of the original question has the advantage of allowing Members to vote against the Estimate, without being compelled to the discourtesy of negativing a grant to the King. More recent editions of May suggest that the real advantage of the procedure is that it allows an indefinite number of varying amounts to be proposed, without first coming to a decision on the original question: which is impossible under the ordinary procedure of the House, because if the House orders words to 'stand part' of a question, they 'stand part' *as they are*, and there is no further possibility of adjustment. Equally if the question that those words stand part is negatived, then the original amount cannot ever be proposed again, and the opportunity of financial adjustment is thus reduced by one item.

Eventually, then, the necessary votes are passed and reported to the House. Consideration ('report stage') of the Supply reports, which must follow, is usually treated as formal, though it is technically open to debate. This is in contradistinction to the report of the Budget resolutions (Ways and Means) which always occasions a real debate.

At about the same time that the Service Estimates are presented, a statement (the Vote on Account) showing the amount of money required to keep the Civil Service departments running from the beginning of the new financial year until the Estimates are finally agreed to is also submitted to Parliament. The statement generally makes allowance for a period of four or five months during which Parliament will be discussing the Estimates. The next business of the Committee of Supply will be to consider a Vote on Account to cover the sum needed for this period. The Vote on Account must be passed before 1 April, since by 31 March all the money Parliament has authorized the Departments to spend will have been spent, or surrendered to the Exchequer again. Without the Vote on Account Whitehall would suddenly find itself without the wherewithal to pay its charladies, and the postmen would find themselves without any wages at the end of the week. The House must therefore consider the

Vote on Account – a process which is exactly similar to the consideration of the Service Estimates. There is no 'moving the Speaker out of the Chair'; that again being reserved for the main estimates.

The First Guillotine. On the seventh of the allotted supply days (or later, but not earlier), the Chairman of Ways and Means rises at 9.30 p.m., calls the Committee to order, and then puts the question on the motion then under discussion without any further debate. He then proceeds to put the question, if it has not already been decided, first of all on the Vote on Account, and on the first votes for the fighting services, on all the supplementary estimates that have been set down for consideration on previous supply days, and finally on any excess votes that there may be.

On the eighth allotted day the resolutions come to in the Committee of Supply are considered 'on report' in the House. At 9.30 p.m., just as in Committee on the previous day, the Speaker rises and puts the question on the resolution under consideration without further debate, and then puts the question on all the other reports from the Committee without debate. Both in Committee and in the House Members may divide against the Government over the sum to be voted but cannot at this stage speak any further for or against it.

This early guillotine, which must take place before 31 March (since it deals with money to be voted for the financial year ending on 31 March, and for the very beginning of the financial year beginning on 1 April) was first instituted in Session 1947–48. Up to 1948 the Government of the day had had to get its votes by 31 March as best it could, though it was assured of getting the main estimates by the operation of the old guillotine in August. Under the new procedure the Government cannot be prevented from getting the necessary votes before the end of the financial year by delaying tactics, though they may of course be defeated.

Ways and Means. It is now the turn of the Committee of Ways and Means. The Committee has to authorize the issue out of the Consolidated Fund of all the sums which have been voted to the service departments and Civil Service by the Committee of Supply, including the supplementary estimates for the financial year now drawing to a close, and excess Votes on financial years long past, besides the Vote on Account and first items of service estimates for the year about to begin. Thus, if the Committee of Supply in February and March 1936 have voted supplementary estimates for the year ending 31 March 1936 amounting to £3,426,845, an excess vote for the financial year ended 31 March 1935 of £1,249 17s. 8d., items of the Estimates for the Army, the Navy, and the Air Force for the financial year ending 31 March 1937, totalling £82,351,900, and a Vote on Account for the Civil Service for the same financial year of £168,890,000, then the Committee of Ways and Means will have to vote a total of £254,669,994 17s. 8d. before the end of March 1936. It will do it in three resolutions; one for the year 1934–35, one for 1935–36, and one for the forthcoming year 1936–37. These resolutions have to be reported to the House in the same way as the report of Supply. Fortunately, as we have seen, proceedings in Committee and report of Ways and Means in its capacity as a spending authority are usually brief and formal.[1]

1. The *modus operandi* is as follows: When the time comes, the Order of the Day for the Committee of Ways and Means, which has been adjourned from week to week ever since the Committee was first set up at the beginning of the Session, will appear on the Order Paper with the words 'to vote a sum out of the Consolidated Fund'. The Order is then 'effective', and when it is read out the House will resolve itself into Committee without question put.

The Consolidated Fund (No. 1) Bill. Approval has now been given (by the Committee of Supply) to the Government to spend money on the public service; and consent has been given (by the Committee of Ways and Means) to issue the required amount from the Exchequer. But still that is not enough. An Act of Parliament must be passed to make all this spending of the nation's money perfectly legal. So the Consolidated Fund (No. 1) Bill is brought in. This is a very brief document. It simply gives to the Treasury power to spend the total of the sums voted in Supply and Ways and Means, and adds power to borrow in anticipation of revenue. The Bill is introduced as soon as the resolutions have been passed in the Committee of Ways and Means and – since it must come into force before 1 April – is passed through all its stages very quickly. But here again debate is not usually of a financial nature. It must be in some way connected with the subject-matter of the expenditure which is being sanctioned: but this obviously embraces a very wide field, and the Consolidated Fund Bills are, like the adjournment, a recognized opportunity for bringing up grievances. For instance, in March 1914 the second reading of the Consolidated Fund Bill was utilized for a long and deeply serious debate on coercion in Ulster (which was then in a state of rebellion). Sometimes, however, the stage of the Consolidated Fund Bill is taken formally and briefly, and the debate is held on a motion for the adjournment of the House. In the case of the final Consolidated Fund Bill, with which the Session closes, Members are at liberty to talk about almost anything they please, so many objects of expenditure are covered by the Bill. If a Session is very long there may have to be another interim Consolidated Fund Bill, which will be called Consolidated Fund (No. 2) Bill; there may be even more than two. In 1943, for instance, there were three Consolidated Fund Bills – owing, of course, to the necessities of war. Usually, however, the second Consolidated Fund Bill does not come on the floor of the House until July or August, and when passed it becomes an Appropriation Act. (There may, in unusual circumstances, be a second Appropriation Act.) This we shall consider in its proper place.

(b) *After 1 April*

Taxation. The Government is now safe, as regards expenditure, for the next few months; and the discussion of the rest of the Estimates can proceed in its leisurely way. Meanwhile, having authorized the issue of money out of the Consolidated Fund, the House now has to consider ways and means of replenishing the Fund, and this it does, appropriately enough, in Committee of Ways and Means.

It should be understood that although almost all the revenue of the Government is derived from taxation, and all taxation must be sanctioned by the House of Commons, most of the taxes which the citizen has to bear are authorized by permanent legislation and do not need to be considered every year. One very important tax, however, is kept on a temporary basis, so that the House of Commons may retain some control over taxation: namely the income tax. This is reimposed every year on the authority of resolutions in Committee of Ways and Means. There used to be other taxes which were kept on a temporary basis. The tea tax, for instance, was debated and reimposed every year, for the same reason, and, at an earlier period, the sugar tax also; but the relative importance of the income tax is now so great that the annual imposition of the tea and sugar taxes has been abandoned. On the other hand, every tax which the Chancellor of the Exchequer proposes to alter in some way, either by increasing the amount or by modifying the manner of assessment, must come before the Committee of Ways and Means again, so that the alterations may receive approval.

The Budget. On a certain afternoon[1] towards the end of April the floor of the House and all the Galleries are packed with people, and an air of unusual excitement pervades the building. There is good reason for the unusual interest: for this is 'Budget night' – the Chancellor of the Exchequer is coming down to the House to move resolutions with regard to the taxes for the new financial year, and, incidentally, to make his great annual statement of the nation's income and expenditure which is known as the Budget Speech. The Budget Speech generally takes several hours to deliver; it is a solemn occasion: it has made or marred great reputations. Gladstone, it will be remembered, made his reputation as a far-sighted Chancellor of the Exchequer. His Budget Speech of 1853, says Lord Morley, 'was one of the great parliamentary performances of the century.'[2] Mr Lloyd George's Budget Speech of 1909, again, was a landmark in social reform. Robert Lorne, on the other hand, made himself ridiculous by his 1871 Budget.

1. On this occasion, Ways and Means appears on the Order Paper together with the words 'Financial Statement' in brackets. This indicates that the Order is now 'effective'; and when it is read out the House immediately resolves itself into Committee without more ado.

2. One recorder who had listened to all the financiers from Peel downwards, said that Peel's statements were ingenious and able, but dry; Disraeli was clever but out of his element; Wood was like a cart without springs on a heavy road. Gladstone was the only man who could lead his hearers over the arid desert, and yet keep them cheerful and lively and interested without flagging. Another is reminded of Sir Joshua's picture of Garrick between tragedy and comedy, such was his duality of attitude and expression; such the skill with which he varied his moods in a single speech, his fervid eloquence and passion, his lightness and buoyancy of humour, his lambent and spontaneous sarcasm. Just as Macaulay made thousands read history who before had turned from it as dry and repulsive, so Mr Gladstone made thousands eager to follow the public balance-sheet, and the whole nation became his audience, interested in him and his themes and in the House where his dazzling wonders were performed.

When the Budget Speech is over there will be speeches of compliment and criticism, and the resolutions (upon which the Chancellor has, theoretically, been speaking) are put to the vote. Some of these must be carried without delay, since they give authority for the increase or diminution of taxation on articles such as cigarettes, in which there may be considerable traffic once the Chancellor has announced what his intentions are. If the tax on beer, for instance, is to be increased, the British public will, as soon as it hears of the projected increase, hasten to lay in beer and the revenue will suffer accordingly. So certain resolutions are passed without delay. They are generally framed in this way: 'That as from the thirteenth day of April, one thousand nine hundred and forty-three, the rate of the duty of excise on sweets shall be increased from one pound three shillings and ninepence to one pound ten shillings per gallon in the case of sparkling sweets, and from eleven shillings and sixpence to fourteen shillings and sixpence per gallon in the case of other sweets.' These resolutions have statutory effect immediately, [1] until the passing of the Finance Act, which will give the new taxation full authority for the rest of the year. The final resolution has of recent years invariably been the 'amendment of law' resolution, which in its usual form is, 'that it is expedient to amend the law with respect to the National Debt and the Public Revenue and to make further provision in connexion with Finance.'

After this motion has been moved the House usually adjourns, [2] and a general debate about the Budget proposals is

1. Under the Provisional Collection of Taxes Act, 1913. A declaration to this effect accompanies each resolution.

2. It was formerly the practice to restrict debate on Budget Night itself to a few complimentary speeches, and to reserve the serious criticism until following days: but of recent years this genial custom seems to have fallen into abeyance.

kept up for the next few days. It will be observed that this arrangement cuts out the possibility of moving practical amendments, which it would be quite in order to make, to the resolutions imposing or altering particular taxes, e.g. to move to leave out the tax on butter. The debate tends therefore to roam rather discursively over the whole field of the Budget Speech.

As soon as the debate is ended, the resolutions which have been passed are reported to the House, and another debate takes place on consideration, when amendments may again be moved. The House then orders the Finance Bill to be brought in, which is done at once. The Finance Bill gives statutory force to the resolutions of Ways and Means, and is based upon them; but it includes the machinery necessary for the various amendments to the laws governing taxation mentioned in the final resolution. So it covers a fairly wide field, and debate upon second reading takes in the whole Government financial policy. It should be remembered that every stage of the Finance Bill is 'exempted business' (as are the Report of Ways and Means resolutions) and each stage must take place upon a separate day. There is thus a good deal of scope for discussion in the Finance Bill, and it may well be July before it is finally passed.[1]

The Appropriation Act. All this time the Committee of Supply

1. In 1909 the Finance Bill was not passed in the Commons until November. Together with the time spent on the resolutions in Ways and Means it occupied no fewer than seventy sitting days. It has been urged (by Mr Kennedy before the 1931 Committee on Procedure) that since the resolutions upon which the Finance Bill is founded have already been discussed in Committee of Ways and Means, and on report, the Committee stage of the Bill should not be taken on the floor of the House. The objection to this is just that there are complicated 'machinery' clauses in the Bill, which are only generally authorized by the resolutions, and that the Committee stage of the Bill itself affords the only opportunity for their discussion in detail.

has been steadily grinding at the main Estimates. Perhaps
'grinding' is not an accurate word: it suggests a minute and
searching examination of the Estimates, and not the most
fervent Parliamentarian would claim that Supply does that.
Twenty-six whole days, as already explained, are allotted
for the discussion of the Estimates each Session (excluding
votes of credit, etc., for war expenditure) and towards the
end of the twenty-six days the House is liable to find itself in
August, with most of the Estimates still undiscussed. Indeed
they will forever remain undiscussed. At 9.30 p.m. (formerly
10 p.m.) on the last allotted Supply day but one the Chairman has to put all the Votes which have not yet been passed,
by classes, and the question on each class must be decided
without debate. All that a critical Member can do is to vote
against an item of which he disapproves; and this process is
sometimes carried to its logical extreme by a vigorous
Opposition – every class is divided on, and the Members
spend hours in tramping through the division lobbies. Then
at 9.30 p.m. on the last allotted day all the resolutions of
Supply which have not yet been reported to the House are
reported, and the same process of clockwork opposition may
be repeated all over again.

All the money thus voted in Supply must be authorized
by corresponding resolutions in Ways and Means; and upon
their being reported to the House the Consolidated Fund
(Appropriation) Bill is ordered to be brought in. This is a
very different affair from the Consolidated Fund (No. 1)
Bill. It enacts that the expenditure which it authorizes is to
be used in exactly the way set out in the schedules – and the
schedules reproduce the Estimates fairly completely, though
omitting some of the lesser detail. It is said to *appropriate* all
the moneys voted to their proper object, and is therefore
sometimes known as the Appropriation Bill, and upon passing, always as the Appropriation Act. The Bill again author-

izes borrowing in anticipation of revenue, and also gives the Treasury power to authorize the service departments in case of need to transfer to one Vote money which has been appropriated to another Vote. This last power ('virement') is given only in the case of the service departments, since their expenditure is of a rather fluctuating and unpredictable kind. The civil departments are expected to keep to the amounts allotted to each Vote; though they can transfer sums of money from one item to another inside each Vote, where there is just cause.

The passing of the Appropriation Act is normally the last piece of financial work which the House is called upon to perform in the Session. It generally comes late in July or even August, and it is permissible, by Standing Order No. 85, to take committee stage and third reading stage in one day. With this the Session usually closes.

*

The Public Accounts Committee. The House has now granted to the Government all the money which it thinks it will need for the year, and has specified (in the Appropriation Act) exactly what the money is to be spent on. It is very careful to do this, since it has had sad experience of the way in which money granted for one purpose can find its way to another object entirely. But it is not enough to say in an Act that the money is to be used for certain purposes. There has to be machinery for ensuring that the money is used in the way that the Act specifies. For this purpose, then, a high officer is appointed, the Comptroller and Auditor-General, whose duty it is to carry out an annual audit of the accounts of Government departments and to report his findings thereon to the House of Commons. The Comptroller and Auditor-General's salary, like that of a High Court Judge, is paid directly out of the Consolidated Fund, not voted every year in Committee of Supply. This is intended to elevate him above politics, and make his criticism independent and fearless.

Each Government department is obliged every year to compile an account of just how it has spent the money voted to it by Parliament; and these accounts, known as Appropriation Accounts – since they deal with the moneys appropriated to the departments by Parliament – are all published, and presented to Parliament together with the reports of the Comptroller and Auditor-General upon them. They follow the form of the Estimates, and they have to show against each item the amount estimated together with the amount actually spent, and the reason for any surplus or deficit.

Long ago it was realized that close scrutiny of public accounts was impossible in a meeting of over 600 Members; and so in 1861, on the motion of Mr Gladstone,[1] a Committee was set up, the Select Committee on Public Accounts – later to become enshrined in the Standing Orders of the House as 'the Committee of Public Accounts'. This body is composed of fifteen members, drawn from all parties of the House, and usually presided over by a prominent Opposition leader, if possible the Financial Secretary to the Treasury of the last Government. The reigning Financial Secretary to the Treasury is also a member.

The Committee sits every week from February until the summer recess, and, in some cases, throughout the Session. It considers the Appropriation Accounts in detail, together with the Comptroller's reports, and summons the accounting officers of the departments to appear and explain any difficulties. These gentlemen – the very highest personages

1. Controversy has raged over the question whether it was Mr Gladstone who originated the Committee of Public Accounts, or not rather Sir Francis Baring who moved for the Select Committee on Public Moneys (a similar body) in 1856. Sir G. Cornewall Lewis was the Chairman of this Committee.

in the Civil Service – foregather in the corridor outside
Committee Room 16 on Tuesdays and Thursdays when the
Committee is sitting, often in an acute and obvious state of
nervousness. The respect and fear entertained in the Civil
Service towards the Public Accounts Committee may seem
out of proportion to its powers. It cannot sentence an
offending official to death: it cannot order torture for an
accounting officer who has lost $3\frac{1}{2}$d.: it can only make an
adverse report to the House. But an adverse report can ruin
a man's career, can provoke a storm in the House. And that
is enough to secure strict adherence to the schedules of the
Appropriation Account.

The Committee is aided in its deliberations by the
Comptroller himself, who sits at the meetings as a part-
member and a part-witness. A high official of the Treasury
also is always present: it is a very efficient tribunal. Many
are the blunders and extravagances which the Public
Accounts Committee has detected, chiefly, of course, in war-
time. The uneconomic expenditure on Naval construction
in 1942–3 and the excessive overdrafts of the British Council
in 1943–4 are cases in point. But there is one feature of its
operations which, from the point of view of securing economy, is a defect. The accounts which it is supervising are
accounts of money which have already been spent, not in the
financial year which has just closed, but in the one before
that. Thus, in 1945, the Committee considered the accounts
for the financial year 1943–4: i.e. for money most of which
had been spent two years before. This is inevitable, since the
accounts cannot be considered until they have been fully
drawn up and reported upon by the Comptroller.

The Estimates Committee. What is needed, then, is supervision,
not of money after it is spent, but of money while it is being
spent and before it is spent. For this purpose, in 1912,

another Committee was set up, the Select Committee on Estimates, to examine the Estimates in detail as soon as they are presented, and to subject them to that kind of searching analysis which is impossible on the floor of the House. In practice it was found that a searching analysis of all the Estimates was not possible in Committee either – the amount of time required, and the complication of the Estimates, were prohibitive. Some scrutiny of the Estimates is attempted: the Committee has been re-appointed every year, except for the war years, and has performed some valuable work. But there is a general consensus of opinion that it was not, before 1939, an unqualified success. The late Sir Malcolm Ramsay, K.C.B., then Comptroller and Auditor-General, in a memorandum submitted to the Select Committee on Procedure of 1931, said, 'The Estimates Committee has, I am afraid, failed to realize the expectations of those who advocated its establishment. It is true that it has helped to secure certain useful improvements, generally of a minor order. But it has effected no substantial economies, and its results have surely been achieved by disproportionate expenditure of time and labour by Members and witnesses, and some at any rate of the matters on which it has made recommendations might equally well have been handled by the Public Accounts Committee (e.g. the re-grouping of Estimates, or the financial control of the Empire Marketing Board).' Ramsay attributed its failure to the obvious facts that the Estimates are for the most part drawn up on the basis of the Government's pre-determined policy; and that it is difficult to interfere with them without entrenching on the Government's right to decide its own financial policy: and indeed the Order of Reference of the Committee is framed to prevent such interference. He also mentions the difficulty of time. The Estimates are presented in February and they must be passed by August: that gives only five months for the

scrutiny of a mass of figures. Finally, he speaks of the difficulty of dealing with the Estimates properly without a large
investigating staff, such as the Comptroller and Auditor-General possesses in the service of the Public Accounts Committee.

During the two world wars the Estimates Committee was
not set up, partly because the scrutiny of the estimating of
various departments was hindered by security considerations. Then the Service Estimates were not published in full,
again for security reasons; only the grand total was issued
to the public. In some cases Parliament voted money as a
Vote of Credit – i.e. a lump sum for unspecified purposes –
which was used to supply the wants of the various mushroom
public departments until they came to be put on a more
permanent basis. Various factors like these made scrutiny of
the Estimates either difficult or useless or both.

In place of the Estimates Committee a Select Committee
on National Expenditure was set up, which formed itself
into sub-committees,[1] and scrutinized with great diligence
various activities of the public departments on which money
was being spent in large amounts, especially where complaints had been received of waste or maladministration.
Accompanied by a devoted staff of clerks the sub-committees went from factory to aerodrome, plumbed the depths
of the earth in mines, and ascended the vistas of the sky in
aeroplanes, investigating personally the work under review,
or sat in the Committee rooms of the House examining,
under conditions of strict secrecy, the officials of the departments responsible. In the course of a few years they produced over a hundred reports on all manner of intricate and
technical subjects, and had, by personal suggestion and persuasion, effected a number of improvements. However

1. The Estimates Committee also had power to appoint sub-committees, but for some reason until 1939 hardly ever did so. Since 1945 it
has regularly done so.

the Committee was confined by its terms of reference to the consideration of war expenditure only, and with the coming of peace it ceased to be appointed.

Some difficulty was found in appointing a successor to this Committee. The essential objection to the old Estimates Committee, namely that it tends to interfere with the running of a department by its responsible head on his own lines, really applies to any Committee appointed to scrutinize Estimates, and is the fundamental difficulty confronting any attempt by Parliament to get the management of the country's finances more effectively under its control. For the moment the Estimates Committee has been set up again with a more adequate staff; but the recent Select Committee on Procedure of 1946 recommended that a single Expenditure Committee combining the functions and the staff of both the Estimates Committee and the Public Accounts Committee should be appointed. It is not at all certain that this recommendation will ever be accepted by either the Government or the House. It has been observed that the amount of actual economy achieved, even by all the sub-committees of the new Estimates Committee does not seem much greater than before. Projects such as the Brabazon aircraft, which cost so many millions of pounds, seem to have avoided any effective public warning. Members, however, seem often to enjoy service on the Committee. It affords them many opportunities of enlarging their knowledge of different matters. Departmental officials will show them round many interesting places. But the Members cannot hope to compete with the technical knowledge of these people. Therein lies the danger. As Ramsay said, such a body as this, investigating matters of policy and reporting upon them publicly may be a real infringement of departmental authority, and a hindrance to the Ministerial conduct of public affairs.

The Public Accounts Committee is, of course, on a very different footing. It has an avowedly post-mortem function. Its business is to scrutinize the Auditor's report on the country's finances. As Lord Kennet has pointed out, the Comptroller and Auditor-General's audit, which is the basis of the Committee's activities, is really an appropriation audit. That is to say, it is his function, not to see that money is spent wisely or well, or even that the accounts presented represent accurately the state of the nation's finance, but to see that the money is spent exactly as Parliament has directed that it shall be spent in the Appropriation Act: and this the Committee certainly does.

The Limits of Control. Now to what extent does the financial procedure which has been described provide an adequate control of the nation's finances? It should be remembered that the nation has nothing corresponding to the balance-sheet of the ordinary commercial firm. It has no comparative account before it of assets and liabilities. All it has is an estimate of the money likely to be required, and an account of the money which has actually been spent, together with a balance of revenue estimated and realized. This is not a method of accountancy which would appeal to a modern business firm. It has been rather rudely described as a 'penny note-book system.'[1]

In the circumstances, the financial control of public expenditure by Parliament must necessarily be very limited. The debates in Supply are, from a financial point of view, admittedly valueless. The work of the Estimates Committee and of the Public Accounts Committee is restricted in the manner just described. All that the nation can be sure of is that money which has been voted for a particular item has

1. See e.g. the Eleventh Report on the Select Committee on National Expenditure, 1945.

been spent on that item: it cannot be sure that it has been spent properly on that item. Moreover, the rigid form of the nation's book-keeping does sometimes result in minor extravagances. The onus of keeping expenditure strictly to the amount voted on each item is so heavy that there is always a temptation to over-estimate, in order to avoid a deficiency, and then to overspend, in order to avoid a surplus, at the end of the year's accountancy. So much is this so that the Treasury has had to issue stringent instructions about settling and deferring matured liabilities to make them fit into a financial year where there is likely to be a surplus or a deficit as the case may be. But it is quite impossible entirely to prevent the manipulating of expenditure to make it agree with the Estimates; and this is not conducive to national economy.

There is another direction in which the finance of the country has escaped almost entirely from the control of Parliament, and that is in the matter of borrowing. A very large part of the revenue goes to pay interest on the National Debt; and this is what is known as a Consolidated Fund Service – i.e. it is paid directly from the Consolidated Fund under permanent legislation, and needs no annual sanction from Parliament. It is true that since it is paid under legislation, and Parliament is the legislature, Parliament must originally have determined that this should be so. But it must be remembered that huge loans raised in time of national emergency and coming eventually to swell the National Debt to fantastic figures are rushed through Parliament on the strength of that national emergency,[1] which

1. E.g. the National Loans Act of 1939, which gave the Treasury power to borrow up to £250,000,000: and the National Loans Act of 1944, which authorized further borrowing up to a year's supply plus £250,000,000. A similar provision occurs in the Miscellaneous Financial Provisions Act, 1946, but other Acts of recent years authorize borrowing far in excess of this – the various Acts to nationalize industry, for instance.

results in a general mitigation of scrutiny: and also that the cumulative effect of several Acts of Parliament, and of many transactions performed under Acts of Parliament, may be very different from what a Parliament would be justified in sanctioning if it had to vote the money annually.

Then it should be understood that a great deal of the nation's affairs are conducted with borrowed money. Quite apart from the sudden crises which demand enormous loans, it frequently happens that the revenue comes in so slowly that loans have to be raised to meet the constant and necessary withdrawals from the Consolidated Fund. Parliament, it is true, authorizes borrowing in the Consolidated Fund Act and the Appropriation Act: but it does not specify the amount, since it cannot foresee what may be needed: it only lays down that it shall not exceed the total sums voted. Moreover it does not specify the rate of interest of the loans, since that depends on the state of the money market: and yet the interest has to be paid.[1] Much the same applies to the huge loans which are raised in war-time, only the interest is much higher.

Inevitably, as expenditure increases, and opportunities for real financial scrutiny diminish, with the increasing

1. See the memorandum submitted to the 1931 Committee on Procedure by Sir Malcolm Ramsay. 'Before 1914 His Majesty's Government could not issue a public loan or borrow money (apart from purely temporary advances) except on the authority of a resolution passed in Committee of Ways and Means (which preceded the issue of the prospectus) and which was the foundation of a Bill giving specific authority for the amount and nature of the issue. But these limitations were swept away by the war, and now ... (1931) ... the Treasury has a general power, until Parliament otherwise determines, of replacing any securities issued during the war.'

On being questioned, Sir Malcolm states, '.... at present the Executive can borrow without the previous consent of the House of Commons up to practically the high-water mark of war-time loans' (q. 3690).

complication of the Estimates, the control of expenditure by the House of Commons becomes less effective. 'The power of the purse,' says Professor Ramsay Muir,[1] in his acid and uncompromising way, 'is supposed to be the main source of authority of the House of Commons. It has become wholly unreal. There is no parliamentary country in which Parliament has less power over finance than in Britain.' Against this one has to remember that as far as honesty and intention is concerned the diminution in the control of the House of Commons has attended a real diminution in the need for such control. The integrity and carefulness of the British Civil Servant is beyond all praise: and there is no better safeguard for economy than an honest executive. Besides, however inflexible our financial procedure may be, it does guard against any peculation or extravagance on a large scale. It is always possible to find out where money is going, though not quite so easy to stop it going there.

'The years during which procedure was being worked out,' says Lord Kennet,[2] 'were the years of struggle between the legislature on the one hand and the Crown on the other. The chief care of the Commons was at first to prevent the Crown from getting money except through Parliament, and in later years to prevent it from spending money on purposes other than those for which Parliament had provided it. Their procedure was planned to act as a check on the Crown in the interests of themselves, the economizers. But times have changed. The rule of Parliament is established, and the power of the Crown is gone. A check upon the Executive's power over the purse is still needed by the Commons as much as ever, but the Executive upon whose power the check has to be exercised is now not the Crown but its

1. In a memorandum laid before the Select Committee on Public Business.

2. E. Hilton Young, *The Finance of Government*, 3rd Edition (1936), p. 42.

Ministers responsible to Parliament. Procedure planned to check the Crown is out of date.'

For that purpose it is certainly out of date. But a new purpose has been found for it. It would be an inestimable gain if the financial procedure of the House could be made an effective control of national finance. But as it stands it is still extremely useful. It provides the cue, on the soundest constitutional basis – that redress of grievances should precede supply of money – for debates which must take place, and which need a motion of sufficient gravity to register the feeling of the House, without tying the hands of the Executive.

CHAPTER VII

LOCAL, PRIVATE LEGISLATION, ETC.

THE Member of Parliament who receives every morning his sheaf of papers from the Vote Office, the Order Paper for the day, the minutes (Votes and Proceedings) of the previous day's Session, and any other documents which he may have ordered, will often find on the top of the sheaf a paper headed 'Private Business'. It contains mostly notices of the various stages of Private Bills set down for consideration that day and corresponds roughly to an Order Paper for local and private legislation.

Just what are Private Bills? We have already seen that they are quite different from Private Members' Bills. We have seen that when a company or a public body needs to acquire land for various purposes, and the owners of the land are unwilling to sell at a reasonable figure, the company or public body will have recourse to a Private Bill; that is, it will come to Parliament and ask for powers to compel them to sell. But this is only one of the most important of the many possible reasons for promoting Private Bills. County Councils and City and Borough Corporations, if they wish to engage in any new undertaking, such as operating an omnibus service, or to spend more of the ratepayers' money on a project than they have previously been authorized to spend, must seek authority from the sovereign power, Parliament: and this is usually done by promoting a Private Bill – though in some cases, under great general Acts of Parliament, certain Government departments have been empowered to give this authority instead. Any body which is already constituted by Act of Parliament (i.e. which has already had to come to Parliament for special powers) must, if it desires to alter its own constitution, or engage in activities not specified in the original Act, promote a Private Bill. Thus, in 1943, when the Grand Union Canal Company wished to form an ocean steamship line of its own, to bring traffic into its canal network, it sought to promote a Private Bill. It had to promote a Private Bill because the builders of the various stretches of canal which formed part of the Grand Union system had had to seek powers of compulsory purchase of land from Parliament in the first place, when they were independent: and when the various Canal Companies were amalgamated to form the Grand Union Canal Company other Acts were passed authorizing the amalgamation. When, in 1943, the London and North Eastern Railway wished to establish a savings bank for its employees on a permanent basis, it had to promote a Private Bill for that purpose. When, in 1943, it was found necessary to apply the enormous funds left by Baron Hirsch for settling Russian Jews in Palestine to another purpose, namely, helping Jews of nationalities other than Russian to settle in Palestine (there being no longer any Russian Jews available for the purposes of the bequest), a Private Bill was promoted in Parliament. When, in 1945, the City of Newcastle-upon-Tyne decided to extend its service of trolley-buses, it applied to Parliament for powers by means of a Private Bill. A Private Bill, then, is a Bill which is designed to further, and which only affects, specific private interests, as opposed to the general classes of the community which are affected by most Public Bills.[1]

---

1. The distinction is not always easy to draw: there are Public Bills which do affect specific private interests, and there are Private Bills which have an effect far exceeding their apparent limits. In the former case, the Public Bill is called a *hybrid* Bill, and goes to the Examiners of Petitions for Private Bills to be examined for compliance with the Private Bill Standing Orders relative to giving notice by advertisement,

A long and interesting history lies behind Private Bill legislation, which would in itself furnish materials for a complete social history of England. There are the Bills of Attainder passed by Plantagenet monarchs with the aim of getting rid of their personal enemies; there are the medieval Bills conferring fishing rights on individuals, or giving local communities powers to put weirs across streams. There are the old Bills giving groups of persons powers to build highways and establish tolls upon them; and Bills empowering private persons to enclose the common land of villages in order to put it under more intensive cultivation – a practice which during the eighteenth century became so popular that in the reign of George III alone no fewer than 1,532 Enclosure Acts were passed, and nearly three million acres enclosed. The eighteenth century saw the beginning of canal building on a large scale, with a consequent spate of Canal Bills, such as the Duke of Bridgwater's great Bill of 1762. In 1801 the first Railway Act, authorizing the building of a track from Wandsworth to Croydon, was passed, and soon the railways had developed to such an extent that the canals were almost obsolete. It was in the first half of the nineteenth century that private legislation reached its peak, with swarms of speculators raising capital to build railroads in every part of the country, and promoting Bills to give their companies statutory existence, and powers of compulsory purchase of land. In Session 1846 no fewer than seven hundred railway Bills were promoted. About this time the great 'battle of the gauges' reached its climax, and a Royal Com-

etc. (see below). The Bill later goes to a small Select Committee, where it is treated as though it were an ordinary Private Bill. It is then recommitted to a Committee of the whole House. The Bank of England Bill is a recent case in point.

Where a Private Bill is found to affect the general interests of the community, it is generally withdrawn, and a hybrid Bill brought in instead.

mission decided, much to the discomfort of posterity, and in the teeth of a contrary recommendation from a Committee of the House, for the narrow gauge. This railway boom was followed by a slump worse than the failure of the South Sea Bubble.[1] Since then the number of Private Bills has progressively declined. The reason is that undertakings which require land for their operations, such as railways, are already fully developed in this country; and that modern commercial enterprise is tending to take forms which do not require much land surface and therefore do not need powers of compulsory land purchase. Another cause of the decline lies in the increasing legislative powers of Government Departments. A great number of general Acts have been passed during the past half-century, giving various Ministers statutory powers to issue Orders which fulfil the same purpose as Private Bills. The most important example of this is the Water Act of 1945. In future, water companies seeking to extend their catchment areas, or asking powers to enlarge their works, will not need to come to Parliament. They can now go to the Minister of Health; and a very considerable (and very contentious) part of private legislation will disappear. Generally speaking, Great Britain is no longer in a condition of industrial expansion, and no longer a country of unrestricted private enterprise. Where powers are required over land, they are usually required by the Government, which has other ways of taking them than by promoting Private Bills. There is indeed a prospect that private legislation may disappear entirely. The Statutory Orders (Special Procedure) Act of 1945 lays down a procedure for dealing with applications from municipal bodies for boundary adjustments, and from companies and

1. A great deal of interesting detail on these matters is given in Clifford's *Private Bill Legislation*, to which I am indebted for the facts cited above.

local authorities for legislation in connexion with the Water Act. Waterworks and Borough Extensions formerly constituted a very large part of private legislation. The absorption of the remainder of private legislation – Company Acts, Private Superannuation Schemes Acts, and the other odd little Acts which fill out each volume of the statute book – by this and similar procedures is perhaps only a matter of time. In the last years before the war there was an annual average of about forty Private Bills; during the war years the number sank to as low as four in one Session; and though it has risen again to about fifty-six in one year (1950), it has fallen again to about thirty-five, and is unlikely to increase much beyond that figure.

Private Bills resemble Public Bills in that most of the work is done before the Bills reach Parliament. There are protracted negotiations, conferences, and disputes between the interested parties. Every effort is made to 'settle' opposition before the Bill is presented, in order to reduce the expense to which parties are liable, which, in the case of contested Bills, is enormous.[1] The Standing Orders of the House of Commons relating to Private Bills are very numerous and complicated, and lay down a strict code of notices by advertisement which must be followed by promoters of Private Bills before the Bills are introduced. In the case of all Private Bills notices must be inserted in the *Gazette* and in the local newspapers of the contents of the Bill. Where land is to be acquired compulsorily all the owners, lessees or occupiers must be notified in writing by a certain date of the intention to take their land. All this is to ensure that all persons likely to be affected by the Bill shall have due warning, and shall be able to oppose it, if they desire, and if they can afford it.

Private Bills differ from Public Bills in that they are pro-

1. See below, p. 242.

moted in the first instance not by Members of Parliament but by outside persons or bodies, acting through a firm of parliamentary agents, and the method of bringing them before Parliament must necessarily be different from that which is followed in the case of Public Bills. In fact the procedure of bringing forward a Private Bill is identical with the practice which in ancient times was followed in the case of all Bills. The promoters present their cases in a petition to Parliament[1] which, however, is not laid on the Table of the House but deposited in the Private Bill Office of the House of Commons on or before 27 November in each Session. Thereafter the agents must appear before the Examiners of Petitions for Private Bills and prove that they have observed all the Standing Orders relative to giving notice to interested persons and the general public. The Examiners are permanent officials appointed jointly by the two Houses, and they make their report to both Houses simultaneously. If the report is favourable the Bills are presented in one or other House[2] within the dates prescribed by Standing Order, and read a first time. In the case of Private Bills, however, presentation and first reading are mere 'book entries', and the Member of Parliament will normally have nothing to do with Private Bills until they come up for second reading, which, in the case of Private Bills originating in the House

1. Until 1675 Members could present Private Bills in the same way as Public Bills. It appears, however, to have been felt that some Members took advantage of this arrangement to promote Bills which their constituents did not really want. Now the only method of presenting a Private Bill is by petition.

2. The Chairman of Ways and Means, and the Chairman of Committees of the House of Lords, acting together, decide which Bills shall originate in which House. Until 1858 all Private Bills originated in the Commons, except for a few personal Bills (Estate Bills, Naturalization Bills, and Divorce Bills). Even now the most important Bills still originate in the Commons.

of Commons, will be at some date in February. In 1950, as the House did not sit until 1 March, after the General Election, the first and second readings were appointed for 9 and 14 March.

Every Member, as we have seen, is kept informed of the progress of Private Bills by a sheet headed 'Private Business'. There he will find the list of second readings, together with the day for which they are set down. He can then, if he feels so disposed, hand in to the table of the House a 'block' – generally a motion that the Bill be read 'upon this day six months,' which, as in the case of a Public Bill, is equivalent to a rejection of the Bill. If there is time, the 'block' will be printed in the next issue of Private Business, but in every case, if a Member has any objection to a Private Bill he has only to stand up when its name is called out for second reading, and say 'Object', and the Bill will be postponed to another day.

Private business is taken during the first five minutes of each day – from about 2.35 to 2.40 (and not after 2.45) or 11.5 to 11.10 (on Fridays). But if a Bill is very strongly opposed, and has been postponed several times, the Chairman of Ways and Means (who is the authority in charge of all private business in the Commons) may direct that it shall be set down for debate on some evening at 7.0. The matter is then thoroughly thrashed out, and the main principle of the Bill approved or disapproved. This arrangement has been much criticized. Important debates – on colonial affairs for instance – have been interrupted at the time of opposed private business, in order that the House might deal with the merits of a measure, say, to allow the City of Hull to make an aerodrome, or to empower the late L.M.S. Railway Company to close down some of its unremunerative canals. This has been represented as incongruous and vexatious. But it is only right, after all, that if Members feel strongly about a Bill which they are asked to pass into law, they should be given an opportunity to state their objections publicly, and be answered in public. At the same time it would not be proper that discussion of this sort should take up the precious time at the beginning of the afternoon, when the maximum number of Members attend. Obviously, a later time in the sitting is desirable, and with the best will in the world it is impossible not to have to interrupt some general debate for it. As a matter of fact it not infrequently happens that the debate on a Private Bill will attract a larger and more attentive audience than a general debate on some topic (such as Africa) of far greater importance though less immediate personal interest to Members. It has been suggested that these debates might well be relegated to a Committee, and not taken on the floor of the House: but that raises the general question whether Private Bills should come on to the floor of the House at all, and there is no doubt that at least the opportunity to take all legislation on to the floor of the House should be preserved if it is humanly possible to preserve it, even if it is necessary to make the use of it more exceptional.

After second reading, Private Bills are committed to a Private Bill Committee.

Opposed Private Bills go to an ordinary Private Bill Committee – a Committee known as a 'Private Bill' group, i.e. a Committee on a group of Private Bills – of four members chosen by the Committee of Selection. Attendance on Private Bill 'groups' is extremely onerous. Members selected must sign a declaration that they are not personally interested in the Bill before the Committee, and that their constituents are not locally affected by it. This declaration is sometimes the cause of much heart-searching. What constitutes personal interest? Ought a debenture holder of a railway company to serve on a Committee on a Bill to authorize a bus service competing with his railway? Ought the Member for Wallsend-on-Tyne to serve on a Committee on a Bill authorizing the extension of the Clyde shipyards? The ramifications of personal interest are endless. But the declaration does not stop there. The Member must promise that he will not 'vote upon any question which may arise without having duly heard and attended to the evidence relating thereto.' This means, in effect, that while the Committee is sitting he must be in attendance all the time. In so small a Committee the constant attendance of all the Members is absolutely necessary: and, if any Member fails to appear at any day's sitting the Chairman is bound, by Standing Order, to report him to the House, which may lead to a public reprimand. Erskine May records the case of one Member who was even committed to the custody of the Serjeant at Arms for neglecting to attend a Private Bill Committee. When it is remembered that a Committee may have to sit upon a Bill for days or weeks it will be readily understood that membership of a 'group' is not much sought after, even though it may lead to the favour of those whose favour is worth having – the leaders of the Party.

What constitutes an opposed Private Bill, and how is it distinguished from an unopposed Private Bill? Simply this. Outside persons who object to a Private Bill on the ground that their property or interests are affected by it, can deposit a petition praying to be heard against it, in the Private Bill Office. They have until 30 January to do this, in the case of Bills originating in the House of Commons, and up to ten days after first reading in the case of Bills brought from the House of Lords, and if by the end of that period no petitions have been deposited against the Bill it is an unopposed Bill and will, on being committed, be referred to the Committee on Unopposed Bills. Many Bills begin by being opposed, and subsequently the opponents withdraw their petitions, as they are quite entitled to do, so that the Bill becomes unopposed. This process of 'settling' is an essential feature of private legislation. Parties deposit petitions against a Bill largely in the hope that the promoters will meet them half-way, by introducing amendments favourable to them, rather than fight the Bill through a 'group', which, as will shortly be seen, is liable to be a rather expensive process. Even at the last minute, when the Committee has already met, parties will 'settle', and the Bill will be withdrawn from Committee. It is only in cases where there is no hope of reconciling the different interests that Bills are taken through a 'group'.

In Committee the semi-judicial nature of private legislation is seen at its plainest. A Committee on a Private Bill is not merely concerned with scrutinizing the details and drafting of the Bill, as a Committee on a Public Bill is or ought to be. Its primary duty is to decide whether the Bill is justified at all: whether the promoters really need it, whether it is the only way of furthering their ends. The Committee must decide whether it is to the public advantage that the Bill should pass into law. Above all, it must assess the claims of the opponents of the Bill who appear before them – the 'petitioners' against the Bill.

Private Bills can readily be distinguished from Public Bills by one salient feature. They all have a *Preamble*, i.e. a paragraph which begins like this:

'Whereas by the Brighton Marine Palace and Pier Act, 1888 (hereinafter referred to as "the Act of 1888") the Brighton Marine Palace and Pier Company (hereinafter referred to as "the Company") were incorporated and authorized (*inter alia*) to make and maintain a promenade pier jetty and landing and shipping place at Brighton with a pier-head or promenade at the seaward end of the pier and to demand and receive certain tolls rates and charges for the use of the said pier and works:

'And whereas by subsequent Acts and by Provisional Orders made by the Board of Trade and by the Minister of Transport respectively under the General Pier and Harbour Act, 1861, the Company have constructed the pier and works authorized by the Act of 1888:

'And whereas the Act of 1888 and the Brighton Marine Palace and Pier Act 1893 (hereinafter referred to as "the Act of 1893") contain provisions with respect to the number and qualification of the directors of the Company:

'And whereas it is expedient that the Act of 1888 and the Act of 1893 should be amended in regard to the matters aforesaid as provided by this Act:

'And whereas it is expedient that the other provisions contained in this Act should be enacted:

'And whereas the objects of this Act cannot be effected without the authority of Parliament:'[1]

The allegations of this preamble the promoters must prove to be true, just as the Crown prosecutor in a criminal case must prove the accused to be guilty. The Committee, in this case, is both judge and jury rolled into one; it hears the cases, assesses the evidence, gives verdict, and decides the sentence, i.e. decides whether, and on what conditions, the Bill shall proceed: what amendments shall be introduced, what clauses struck out. The sort of things which a Private Bill seeks are what in any other country would be applied for to the law courts or to the executive. Only in England and the Dominions is the right of free approach to

---

1. This is followed by the *enacting formula:*

'May it therefore please Your Majesty that it may be enacted and be it enacted by the King's most Excellent Majesty by and with the advice and consent of the Lords Spiritual and Temporal and Commons in this present Parliament assembled and by the authority of the same as follows (that is to say)' and then by Clause I, the 'citation' clause.

Parliament on the part of private individuals still preserved.

The proceedings of a 'group' are much more elaborate
and impressive than those of the Unopposed Bill Committee,
of which more anon. All petitions against a Bill are automatically referred to the Committee on the Bill; and both
sides – the promoters and the petitioners – brief counsel to
represent them. The *mise-en-scène* is very picturesque. The
Committee sits in a semicircle at one end of the room, while
across the other end of the room, at a long table, the various
counsel, in wigs and gowns, are seated:

> 'Deep on their front engraven
> Deliberation sit and public care.'

Behind them, and round the edges of the court, surges a
throng of agent's clerks, witnesses, officials of the bodies involved, representatives of Government departments.[1]
Counsel rise and address the Committee in turn and at
length: other counsel rise to points of order, or to correct 'my
learned friend in the statement he has made'; solemn alter-
cations arise; heavy legal jokes ripple the somnolent gravity
of the other counsel. The counsel for the promoters produces
incontrovertible arguments to show that unless his Bill is
passed all the inhabitants of their town will languish of
thirst; the counsel for the petitioners points out, with equally

1. The promoters of the Birmingham Corporation Bill, 1945, produced as part of their case in Committee a large scale model of the city of
Birmingham. This, with the vast attendance of counsel, witnesses, and
spectators, made it impossible to find a room to contain the Committee
in reasonable comfort. For a time, use was made of the large room 14,
until it was needed for a Standing Committee: and for a fortnight the
proceedings took place in conditions of acute discomfort in an ordinary
committee room. The attendance during the sittings of the Committee
rose at times to between 60 and 100 people.

compelling logic, that if his learned friend is allowed to proceed with his impounding scheme all the rivers in the
petitioners' area will cease to flow and navigation on the
lower reaches will become impossible. While the Committee
are pondering these conflicting statements, witnesses are
produced, who swear that the inhabitants of Wisbech are
so short of water that the supply is turned off twice a day
and, on the other hand, that water is more plentiful there
than anywhere else in the country.

If this is exaggeration, it does at least convey the atmosphere of the Committees. They are legal tribunals, and
they have to listen to the arguments of trained advocates
presenting the case of their clients in the strongest light.
However strange the conflict of opinion may appear to the
visitor, and however elaborate he may find the process of
argument, he must remember that human argument is often
involved and heated over matters which appear insignificant to the bystander, and that the Private Bill group has
been found in the course of centuries to be the most satisfactory way of dealing with such matters. It is hardly necessary to remind the reader of the various war-criminal trials
in Germany to bring out the point that what appears on
prima facie evidence to be a straight issue between right and
wrong may have ramifications of the most complicated
character, and take a great deal of time to disentangle.

After sitting on a few such Committees Members begin to
realize that the faces and voices of some of the witnesses are
strangely familiar to them. In the fulness of time they discover that there is a class of professional witnesses, even as
there is a class of professional advocates, and that these
eminent persons make a considerable part of their living by
attending to give Committees the benefit of their experience
and training in a particular field – why not? These persons,
being well trained, are not likely to be shaken or confused

in their plain statements by the irony or the rigour of the cross-examination.

At the end of the evidence, the learned counsel sum up their respective cases, ending with the speech of the counsel for the promoters, who thus has the first and last say[1] – and rightly, since on him rests the onus of proof.

After counsel have finished, the room is cleared, and the Committee deliberate. They have to decide (a) whether the promoters have made out their case – i.e. whether to pass the Bill; (b) if so, whether there are any conditions which must be imposed upon the promoters, and any major amendments which must be inserted. This done, parties are called back into the Committee room and informed of the Committee's decision. The decision takes the form of an announcement that the Committee find the preamble proved, or do not find the preamble proved, as the case may be: for the preamble is the hinge upon which, in the majority of cases, all the speeches of counsel and all the evidence turn. If the preamble is not proved, there is an immediate end of the Bill: nothing remains but to report it without amendment back to the House. If the preamble is proved, most of the counsel and their satellites withdraw, and the remaining points which need explanation are dealt with in a less formal way by the counsel for the Bill – or, more frequently, by the senior partner of the parliamentary agents for the Bill. It is at this point that representatives from Government departments are called upon to amplify the reports upon the Bill which their Minister has submitted to the Committee. It is at this point that a great many rather important and (sometimes) unusual clauses may be passed with very little scrutiny. The Committee are responsible for

1. But the counsel for the promoters has this last say only where evidence has been called by the petitioners – i.e. where new facts have been brought to the attention of the Committee.

everything in the Bill: but the system of consideration of a Bill in Private Bill group, with argument by counsel only on points rousing heavy opposition, tends to focus and exhaust the attention of the Committee on the points in dispute; whereas other parts of the Bill, equally important, but not the subject of local opposition, often do not receive the attention they deserve. This is unfortunate since it results in a lack of uniformity in legislation. Occasionally different promoters of the same type of Bill favour different kinds of regulations on the same matters: and thus in different parts of the country the law with regard to, let us say, sewers and water-mains is sufficiently different to cause confusion, and make the task of general legislation more difficult.[1]

One point which should be remembered by all Members serving on Committees on Private Bills is that such Committees have no power to summon witnesses themselves. Evidence is produced by the various parties, just as in a civil action in court: and the Committee must decide the question on the evidence before them. Consequently officials of Government departments are not entitled to speak to the Committee except briefly in amplification of their report on the Bill. If it is absolutely essential for a Committee to summon witnesses itself it must get the House to make an order for the attendance of those witnesses: but this is never in fact done.

All minor points having been cleared up, the Bill is signed by the Chairman, and reported to the House in 'dummy', just as in the case of a Public Bill. Consideration stage

1. The position is somewhat alleviated (a) by the existence of standard clauses on a large variety of subjects, of which the draftsmen of Private Bills make use, and (b) by the scrutiny which the Speaker's Counsel brings to bear on all Private Bills, and the guidance which he is able to give to the authorities of the House, and in particular to the Chairman of Ways and Means, who, as has been pointed out, is in a position of control over all private legislation.

('report stage') follows, and then third reading. In each case Members can object in the House, and the Bill may be defeated; and on consideration stage new amendments may be proposed, just as in the case of a Public Bill. After third reading the Bill passes to the other House, and in due course, if no mishap occurs, becomes an Act.

Private Bills which are unopposed go to an Unopposed Bill Committee, consisting of five members[1] *plus* the Counsel to Mr Speaker. The proceedings of this Committee are usually brief and sometimes only formal. The senior partner of the firm of parliamentary agents who are handling the Bill appears before the Committee, explains the general purpose of the Bill, accounts for any clauses of an unusual nature, and produces formal evidence (from the Town Clerk in the case of a borough Bill, or from the company solicitor in the case of a company Bill) that the preamble is true. Actually, most of the work will have been done already by the Speaker's Counsel and the Agents in private conference. The Committee must, nevertheless, satisfy itself that the Bill follows precedent, or does not depart from precedent without good reason; and must take particular care to see that the expediency of the Bill is proved to them.

From what has been said it will be realized that the promotion of Private Bills, especially opposed Private Bills, is by no means a pastime for a poor man. The grave and learned counsel expect a fee ranging from £200 upwards; the expert gentlemen mentioned above, who are annual visitors to the Committee rooms, require to be reimbursed for their pains on a scale which ordinary people might consider generous. Then there are the cloud of witnesses, agent's clerks, borough officials. All these must be paid for by the

1. Namely, the Chairman of Ways and Means (who rarely attends), the Deputy Chairman (usually Chairman of the Committee), and three members chosen by the Chairman.

promoters and their opponents. In the case of local authority
Bills the expense falls on the public – that is, on the ratepayers; in the case of statutory companies such as water
companies the cost will have to be borne by the public, since
the company is usually paying its authorized dividend, and
the costs of the Bill will have to be met by an increase in the
charges to the consumer.[1] The actual total, of course, varies
immensely. One Bill in Session 1927 cost the promoters over
£17,000; another in Session 1928 cost over £11,000, and in
the end did not become law. On the other hand ten Bills
which were promoted in the same Session cost less than
£1,000 each: some of them very much less than £1,000.[2]
The difference is largely between opposed and unopposed
Bills, and arises from the expense of the Committee stage in
the case of opposed Bills. The Dunnico Committee estimated
that Counsel's fees amount to about 28 per cent of the total,
in the case of Bills opposed in both Houses; and that fees
paid to experts formed the majority of the remaining cost.
This Committee, which was set up in 1930, had, as one of
its objects, the reduction of expense of private legislation:
but they were unable to suggest any notable economies.
Legislation and litigation are very similar in this respect. It
is almost impossible to make them cheap, and not wholly
certain that it would be desirable to make them cheap if it
were possible.[3]

1. Sir Frederick Liddell, giving evidence before the Dunnico Committee, H.C. 158, 1930, p. 49.

2. Figures quoted from the Dunnico Report. The cost of private
legislation at the time of the railway boom was far greater. From the
Third Report of the Select Committee on Private Bills, 1847, we learn
that the preliminary expenses of the Direct Northern Railway, before it
even went into Committee, were £123,414: and the expenses of the
London and York Railway Bill, over two Sessions, were £309,206.

3. It would probably be impossible to promote a Private Bill, even if
unopposed, for less than £400 at present rates.

Private legislation is not a poor man's pastime, and equally it is not a layman's pastime. It is open to anyone to deposit on his own account a petition for a Bill or a petition against a Bill: but unless he is unusually gifted it would be very inadvisable for him to do so. The steps which have to be taken in connexion with Private Bills; the people who must be informed; the documents which must be deposited; the negotiations which must be undertaken; all this is so complicated that no one but an experienced parliamentary agent could hope to deal with it successfully. Private persons have from time to time within recent years deposited petitions against Bills on their own account in Parliament; but owing to their inexperience have achieved little by their pains.

Provisional Order Bills

To a certain extent in England already, and almost wholly in Scotland, Private Bills have been superseded by Provisional Order Bills. These are Bills to confirm 'orders' made by some Government department. The company or the town council, as the case may be, approach a Government department for an Order authorizing them to do what would otherwise have to be authorized by Private Act. The department then usually holds a local inquiry, and, if it is satisfied that the application is justified, issues the Order, and presents a Bill in Parliament, by means of its Minister, to confirm the Provisional Order. Most of the work has thus been done before the Bill (which is called a Provisional Order Bill) reaches Parliament, and almost all Provisional Order Bills are unopposed, and pass very quickly and comparatively inexpensively. Their passage through the House is not impeded by the Standing Orders which apply to a Private Bill. If, however, parties decide to oppose a Provisional Order Bill in Parliament, by petition, the process can become just as long and as costly as an opposed Private Bill, or rather more costly, since in the case of the Provisional Order Bill expenses have already been incurred on the initial local inquiry. The procedure under the Statutory Orders (Special Procedure) Act (see below) was intended to take the place of Provisional Orders altogether, and has to a certain extent done so.

Procedure under the Statutory Orders (Special Procedure) Act, 1945
Some mention has already been made of this Act as threatening the entire extinction of Private Bill procedure as we know it. At first it applied only to orders made under three or four Acts, and dealt mainly with water supply schemes and local government boundary adjustments. But in 1949 an Order extended its powers to cover the field of Provisional Orders, and the scope of the procedure has been applied to more and more subjects. On the other hand, Local Government boundaries are no longer subject to these Orders. So it will be as well to give a brief outline of the procedure as it is intended to operate.

First of all, then, the individual parties in these matters approach the department, just as in the case of a Provisional Order. There will be preliminary proceedings, just as in the case of a Provisional Order, and a local inquiry. Then, if the department is satisfied, an Order will be laid on the Table of each House of Parliament.

After this a period of fourteen days elapses, during which (1) a Member of either House may move in the House that the Order be annulled, or (2) parties objecting to it may petition against it.

If neither of these contingencies occurs, the Order will become operative without further proceedings. If, on the other hand, petitions for amendment of the Order are lodged against it, it will have to go to a Joint Committee of both Houses, which will function like a Private Bill 'group'. The Committee will then report to Parliament, and the Order will become operative with any amendments which the Committee have suggested.

The Statutory Orders (Special Procedure) Act received the Royal Assent only in December 1945, and up to the time of writing comparatively few Orders, mostly un-opposed, have been made under it. It will be interesting to see how this very expeditious procedure works out in the end. So far the Special Procedure Orders have dealt mainly with water, navigation and compulsory purchase of land.

CONCLUSION

I T will not be imagined that the foregoing account of the procedure of the House of Commons is in any sense exhaustive. Even the thousand pages of Erskine May are not exhaustive. The only *exhaustive* account of procedure is to be found by a study of May in conjunction with all the volumes of the *Journal*, of *Hansard*, of the *Parliamentary History*, of Symonds D'Ewes and of innumerable other works. Such an account would be found to be not merely exhaustive but exhausting. All that could be attempted here was to give an accurate, detailed and, for the immediate purpose, comprehensive survey of the work and working of the House as it was likely to come before the reader, or affect the Member.

It will nevertheless be felt by many readers even of this brief review that parliamentary procedure is overwhelmingly, even absurdly, complicated. That is, to some extent, a correct impression. The very antiquity of procedure tends naturally to make it complicated. The vast diversity of topics to be handled, of situations to be dealt with, renders it still more complicated. Procedure designed to meet every contingency cannot be simple.

So much being admitted, the question arises whether this complexity is in every case necessary. Cannot our procedure be simplified? Are there no directions in which reform is possible?

Undoubtedly there are many features of the procedural landscape which arouse misgivings. The present Supply machinery is in very much the same position as was the English electoral system before the Reform Bill. It contains many grotesque features, entails many incidental advantages, and largely fails to perform what it is apparently intended to perform. Again, the Order Paper is literally un-intelligible to a large number of Members. But it is one thing to point to defects, and quite a different matter to say how they should be remedied. Within the past two decades two Select Committees have been appointed with just this object in view – to examine procedure, and to find out what improvements, if any, were needed in it. The findings of those two Committees are of the greatest interest. But the changes they have recommended are to the outward eye insignificant.[1] The fact is that any really far-reaching over-haul of procedure would entail laying sacrilegious hands upon the vital principles of that intangible creature, the British constitution; and no Select Committee has so far been empowered, or expressed the desire, to attempt that.

Improvements have been made from time to time, and will continue to be made. Perhaps in time some courageous Government will feel inclined to tackle the fundamentals of the Supply position. Perhaps the lush undergrowth of the Order Paper will be cut back and weeded. Meanwhile it is of importance that every effort should be made to explain the workings of this great machinery to the public. If the present author has been in any way successful in elucidating a part of what the reader wanted to know about the House of Commons, or in stimulating his desire for further know-ledge, he has fulfilled his own highest expectations.

August 1951

1. It is only fair to point out that the Select Committee on Procedure of 1945–46 was chiefly concerned with making procedure more speedy and efficient, not primarily with making it simpler. In some cases, efficiency may entail more complication, not less.

SELECT BIBLIOGRAPHY

It is impossible to give here a full bibliography of books on Parliament, or even of the works mentioned in this book. The essence of the subject is contained in the following books:

Manual of Procedure in the Public Business. Laid on the Table by Mr Speaker for the use of Members. Eighth Edition, 1951.

This is the only *official* work on parliamentary procedure. It was originally compiled by Sir Courtenay Ilbert, and has now been re-issued by the Clerk of the House, Sir Frederic Metcalfe, K.C.B. It is a most valuable brief guide. (H.M. Stationery Office, 7/6.)

The Law, Privileges, Proceedings and Usage of Parliament, by Sir Erskine May. Fifteenth Edition, 1950, edited by Lord Campion and T. G. B. Cocks.

This is generally regarded as the authoritative work on the subject. But it is not an official publication, although it is frequently cited as such. The arrangement of this work was perhaps inferior in its original conception to its American equivalent (Cushing's *Law and Practice of Legislative Assemblies in the United States of America*), a very useful work, which however was written after, and probably with the assistance of, May's book. (Butterworth & Co, Ltd, 75/-)

An Introduction to the Procedure of the House of Commons, by Lord Campion, G.C.B. Second Edition, 1947. Now reprinted with corrections.

This book is not recommended to the casual reader without preliminary training. (Macmillan & Co, Ltd, 18/-)

Procedure of the House of Commons, by Joseph Redlich, 1908. A useful historical survey.

Parliament, by Sir Ivor Jennings. A lively book by a distinguished constitutional lawyer (Cambridge University Press, 1939, 25/–).

Hansard, The Official Report (verbatim) of debates in Parliament, published by H.M. Stationery Office. Daily parts of the House of Commons Debates, 9d., the '*Weekly Hansard*', 2/–.

Journals of the House of Commons. Published annually by H.M. Stationery Office, on the orders of the House of Commons. Large, expensive volumes: not of interest except to the specialist. The Journals record the minutes of the House, in a more expanded form than Votes and Proceedings, still in eighteenth or even seventeenth century prose. They go back to the sixteenth century, and have annual and decennial indexes.

INDEX